Praise for Balance

This book puts all the everyday decisions of a sch... perspective we can all relate to. I wish I had the book when I first became a principal. It is so easy to get caught in the emotion of a situation, especially when it is delicate and involves parents or staff. Andrew provides realistic scenarios and level-headed strategies to deal with situations where the question is: "Do I stick to protocol, or do I build a relationship here?".

Gabrielle Hansen,
Head of Department – Curriculum

The spread of chapters and topics is a wonderful resource for principals working through the five P's process and offers a reaffirmation of current principal practices that may spark change in future practice. The insights shared in this book support both new and experienced principals to navigate their daily work. The scenario reflection section at the end of each chapter is a good idea for leaders. Also, the three questions for productive parent-teacher communication is a great tool for school leaders.

Kurt Rose, principal

Andrew Oberthur has done it again. He has taken on one of the world's most complex and challenging human dynamics: how do we manage the relationships of teachers, parents and primary school students to produce a significant improvement in our educational outcomes? The book is enriched with real-life examples from day-to day-happenings of what does work, what could work and what doesn't work that leave the reader thinking, "Oh, yeah. That's obvious; yet I would never have thought of it".

Allan Parker OAM, behavioural
scientist and international negotiator

This book is a worthwhile resource and of particular interest to early career principals as they navigate the complex world of principalship. Andrew has thought of many scenarios which are pertinent and relevant in the decision-making processes of school leaders.

Kerry Latimer, retired principal

Andrew Oberthur hits some of the major themes that school leaders face in finding the balance between following the rules and adopting a level of flexibility. I also feel that he cautions, covertly, regarding the things you can't be flexible around and why. Andrew finds a good balance (no pun intended) between writing about state and independent systems. Finally, I think the question he poses early, "Does this improve the learning and wellbeing of students, staff and families?", provides a solid ethical and moral foundation on which principals and school leaders can base their decisions.

Ray Boyd, principal

BALANCE

BALANCE

Building Positive Relationships
within Educational Protocols

Andrew Oberthur

amba
press

Published by Amba Press
Melbourne, Australia
www.ambapress.com.au

Editor – Beth Browne
Cover Designer – Alissa Dinallo

Printed by IngramSpark

ISBN: 9781922607263 (pbk)
ISBN: 9781922607270 (ebk)

A catalogue record for this book is available from the National Library of Australia.

CONTENTS

FOREWORD

This is the second book by Andrew Oberthur which I have had the pleasure of reading. The books offer deep, but simple, insights into issues which affect us all, particularly in relation to apparent problems in educating young people, both formally and informally.

This current book reflects on some peculiar conditions resulting from the COVID-19 pandemic and the effects of its official handling by relevant authorities for future enlightenment. If nothing else, the pandemic period should have taught us how frail are our rights and how fragile are our leaders when we fail to ask "why?". This question is omitted in many educational reviews which focus on what and when. This book also deals with why and how, the necessary ingredients in education for responsible citizenship.

Thus, the goals of the author remain "for children to be confident contributors to society" and "for teachers and parents to be engaged collaboratively in their children's learning journey". While no-one could object to these, this book is different from many others in that its first seven chapters are filled with very practical wisdom based on the author's extensive experience in partnering children and their parents and encouraging parents to engage in such partnerships. Long gone are the days when teachers felt that parents had done their job when they had brought their children into the world and then delivered them to the schooling system five years later to be left in the hands of the experts.

The last three chapters also build on the first seven with practical guidance on Behaviour Management, Cultural Diversity and Managing Through Uncertainty, all of which would help most office environments that I have encountered, particularly with their practical scenarios, dilemmas, options and response choices. These chapters, particularly in conjunction with the diagrammatic summaries in the appendices, would apply to the communication dynamics of any business office. Thus "the conditions necessary for children to learn" are the conditions necessary for adults to cooperate and communicate. Similarly, the formula for trust and collaboration has potential for widespread commercial application through continuing professional development in any business office. In the same sense, this trust model for parents and teachers can be translated into a model which works for clients and customer staff, as it is the human factors which can enrich or inhibit the transaction irrespective of the quality of the product.

The product for the author of course is the well-rounded pupil who has met the parents' and teachers' challenges as he or she has developed. Thus, the final appendix returns to the school environment with a useful summary sample of school issues that could be managed under each of the criteria elaborated in the book.

The contents of the book are challenging for teachers, parents and children engaged in a mutual triple partnership for the good of each and for the benefit of the society where they live and work. The author covers creativity, character and citizenship in some detail, including the effects of middle class piling of pressure on children by project managing parents: let children be children! All readers will be able to relate to the neatly explained examples, which are up to date in terms of what children are exposed to in the media, both new and old, and how adults can underestimate what children already know before their parents get around to thinking about telling them.

The author's goals in writing this book work because the narrative is built around realistic case studies which reinforce the points he is making. Some of the case studies are from the author's own experience, while others are from experts around the world. This makes the book valuable reading for a variety of audiences, since we all need expressions of our love to be reinforced frequently and in simple ways; and, as suggested, there are serious discussions which can apply to any working context. These are presented in an engaging and enjoyable discourse with the reader.

Emeritus Professor Tony Shannon AM

ACKNOWLEDGEMENTS

In writing this book I was conscious to make it relevant for a wide range of school teachers and school leaders. To achieve this, I sought the wisdom of friends and colleagues in a variety of education sectors. I thank my colleagues Rob Amedee and Kerry Latimer, retired principals, who read an early draft of the manuscript and gave me some key feedback. Similarly Gabby Hansen, Kurt Rose and Ray Boyd gave me some critical feedback from their viewpoint in their education sector. I thank them for their ideas.

I thank my trusted friend and mentor, Allan Parker OAM, who always brings clarity to my writing, for his guidance and challenging questions.

Having someone of the calibre of Professor Tony Shannon read my work and bring his wealth of experience to add to the quality of the content is invaluable. I thank Tony for his time and thoughts and for writing the foreword.

My career with Brisbane Catholic Education has spanned over 33 years. In this time I have worked with many teachers, teacher aides, colleagues and educational leaders. Every interaction, especially in the last few years, has allowed me to reflect on the work and the outcomes. I say thank you to my colleagues who have inspired me, who have shared stories and who have added to my professional journey. The conversations we have had have brought a depth to my experiences, some of which are recalled in this text.

I thank my family – Lisa, Zac and Bridget – for their patience when writing absorbed my mind and time. Their words of support are appreciated.

Finally, I thank Alicia Cohen, my trusted publisher, for her words of advice, encouragement and wisdom. Her faith in my writing kept me going when it became "too hard" on some occasions.

I hope this book adds to the dialogue around school leadership and prompts conversations among leaders so together we can provide high-quality education while remaining true to our core business, meeting our legal and ethical obligations and building positive relationships with those whom we work with and educate.

INTRODUCTION

If you had to choose between following your school's rules to the letter or breaking them in the best interests of human relationships, what would you do? How would you choose? Would you let your head rule your heart or vice versa? Or would you try to find a balance between building positive, harmonious and productive relationships and working within the rules and regulations under which all schools function? The aim of this book is to explore that exact dilemma. How do school leaders and teachers negotiate and navigate the minefield that is following rules while fostering positive relationships?

Schools function according to numerous protocols, practices, procedures, processes and policies (which I'll refer to as the five P's in this book) while navigating the core business of education which is teaching and learning. The five P's are designed to guide the school community to function efficiently; to keep people safe; to provide a culture of trust, collaboration and enquiry; and to create a high-performing school. Relationships within schools should be built and developed to create the same culture with the same end goal.

On occasions there is a tension, a balancing act, between following the five P's and building positive, harmonious relationships. The two can work hand in hand and do not need to be mutually exclusive. There are numerous examples of such tensions in society, business, history, sport, education, music and politics – which are often reported in the media, movies and literature as well as by relationship and leadership experts – where a balancing act between following protocols and fostering positive relationships is required. When relationships and the five P's intersect and create tension, school leaders need to manage the balancing act. They can and they do!

This book focuses on how educational leaders and teachers manage their relationships with students, parents and each other within school protocols. Its premise is not that school leaders and teachers need to choose between working with the five P's *or* building relationships; it is rather about *how* to balance both. As Hargreaves and O'Connor (2018) remind us, we need both in our professional life and we need a way to use the best of both worlds. Teachers who can collaborate in a professional sense have strong relationships but also use the tools, structures and protocols necessary for continuous improvement in their school. We will unpack this model and more in Chapter 5.

There is no easy answer. There is no one-size-fits-all solution. What we have are real-life examples that school principals, deputies and teachers must navigate on a regular basis. Building a culture of trust and collaboration requires experience, wisdom and a transparent rationale. It is this culture that results in a balance between honouring and following protocols while appreciating the importance of relationships between all stakeholders in a school community.

Throughout the book I refer to popular movies where characters were required to make choices around building and maintaining positive relationships within protocols. Some are good examples of balancing relationships and protocols, while others are examples of what can go wrong. Many of these films are based on true stories where accepted protocols had to be challenged to promote positive relationships. Some of them remind us that brave decisions by individuals to challenge protocols in favour of building relationships, both personally and collectively, can change history. Many successful people have achieved greatness in their fields by stretching the accepted norms of their profession or society. Some of these people placed more emphasis on building their relationships with others or their culture while respectfully challenging the five P's.

The American writer Malcolm Gladwell, author of *Outliers* (2008), explores conditions which may be common for people achieving success which is outside the norm – that is, the extraordinary success of individuals, many of whom changed the world. He proposes that "[t]heir world – their culture and generation and family history – gave them the greatest of opportunities" (p. 158). These successful people often operated outside the protocols or stretched the accepted norms to achieve greatness. Their success was rarely solo. Their connections often enhanced their relationships, both personal and professional. Gladwell contends that "if you work hard enough and assert yourself, and use your mind and imagination, you can shape the world to your desires" (p. 151).

Looking further afield from the school context, the rationale for balancing relationships within protocols is relevant in many industries, especially those that work towards improving the world. Balancing protocols and relationships does not mean you sit in either camp; rather it means you operate somewhere along the continuum for each separate negotiation (because, as my friend and mentor Allan Parker reminds me, every human interaction is a negotiation). Community leaders face this balancing act on a regular basis. Some decisions will have tremendous significance, while others will have less impact on the world around them. Some industries have protocols that are a matter of life and death. In such fields, deviating from the protocols is rarely an option. Flying a plane and performing surgery are examples where protocols must be followed and where virtually all contingencies are practised to ensure the safety of all involved. (Note the word "safety" – it is highly relevant and discussed in detail later in this book).

Mike Lotzof, author of *Legal but Harmful* (2017), analysed the behaviours of cultures and corporations around the world that were technically legal yet harmful. He found society is littered with examples of such behaviour. Some laws that existed historically have since been changed to comply with discrimination legislation (see Chapter 1).

Similarly, there are many examples throughout history where laws and societal rules endorsed discriminatory behaviour or harmful relationships until someone was brave enough to challenge, bend, break or create new protocols that promoted equity and positive relationships.

The 2018 film *On the Basis of Sex* explores a number of historical protocols that were legal yet harmful. The film tells the story of Ruth Bader Ginsburg, one of America's finest lawyers and one of Harvard Law School's first female graduates, from the late 1950s to the early 1970s. Throughout her education and career, Bader Ginsburg experienced many forms of discrimination.

While studying at Harvard, and when her husband was in remission from cancer, Bader Ginsburg sought permission from the dean to transfer to another university, which would have been more convenient for her family in case her husband had a relapse. In a clear example of protocols overruling relationships, the dean declined, citing his desire to not undermine the value of Harvard's law degree.

When Bader Ginsburg was presented with a sex discrimination case she wished to defend, she approached a male colleague who ran a large law firm to underwrite the case. He was reluctant, reminding her that "morality does not win the day". The case was to challenge a law that prevented single men from accessing the same tax benefits as married men who were caring for ailing parents or spouses. She felt the law was wrong and offered to take on the defence pro bono. Bader Ginsburg and her husband co-presented the case and won.

The law at the time was considered just according to society's standards. When one of the three judges hearing the case asked Bader Ginsburg if she wanted the judges to go against 100 years of precedent, she replied, "I am asking you to set a precedent". In effect, she was challenging society's expectations of roles and entitlements based purely on gender. Bader Ginsburg subsequently became a leading figure in cases of discrimination based on gender. As described in the movie, she made "radical cultural change".

David Epstein's *Range* (2019) highlights how generalists survive and thrive in a specialised world. He recounts various stories where individuals had to balance relationships within the protocols. Some of the fascinating stories provide other evidence as to how people juggle the balancing act of promoting positive relationships within protocols. Specialisation is like following the five P's, where people follow the rules, while generalists may have breadth of thought and are open to new possibilities, including building relationships outside the five P's. Andy Ouderkirk was an inventor at Minnesota-based company 3M who believed that "working on well-defined and well-understood problems, specialists work very, very well. As ambiguity and uncertainty increases, which is the norm with systems problems, breadth becomes increasingly important" (Epstein, 2019). Schools are an environment where a degree of ambiguity and uncertainty exist frequently.

Many professions have numerous guidelines, frameworks, regulations, rules, policies, practices, procedures, processes and protocols that leaders may draw upon when making decisions. Such decisions are not always a matter of life and death and, as such, the leader and others may have a degree of discretion in how they engage or how they act to enhance human relationships. Education is one such profession that is drowning in frameworks while requiring leaders and teachers to build positive relationships within their communities.

School leaders bring their own values to their schools, and they are expected to act in an ethical manner when making decisions. However, where do school leaders' values, which allow them to make ethical decisions, come from? According to storyteller, podcaster and former monk Jay Shetty (2020), "our values are influenced by whatever absorbs our minds" and "the mind is the vehicle by which we decide what is important in our hearts". This is a compact way of explaining the rationale for this book. How do school leaders use their minds – the five P's – to make decisions, and how do they use their hearts to build relationships in their schools? More precisely, how do school leaders balance their hearts and their minds when making decisions?

Working within the five P's – understanding what is expected and the likely outcomes of behaviours – gives people confidence in the leaders of their context, and this applies to the school environment as well. Teachers, parents and students appreciate consistency in responses and transparency of processes. They appreciate clear rationales for decisions and actions, both reactive and proactive. There will be times when decisions are made by a principal without a public rationale. These decisions are largely accepted when the principal and their leadership team have "runs on the board" and a solid balance in the emotional bank account of the school community. Let me explain. If a person does a good thing for another person, that creates an emotional credit in the relationship between the two people. And the more emotional credits are created through positive interactions, the more latitude is given when harsh decisions need to be made.

When leaders who have made wise decisions that have benefited the community over a period of time are required to make a harsh decision, which may have a perceived or actual negative impact on people, the public are more likely to be gracious in their acceptance if the emotional bank account is in credit. Through making such decisions, people go into credit with positive relationships. This can be on a one-on-one relationship, it can be an individual to a group relationship or it can be one party to a larger group of people. You also build up credit through trust, through consultation and collaboration, and through asking questions and seeking opinions of others.

The advantage of working collaboratively in a leadership team is that each member of the team brings strengths which ideally balance the importance of following protocols and the importance of building relationships.

When making decisions in the best interests of students, staff and families, the key question that we as school leaders and teachers should keep at the forefronts of our minds is:

Does this improve the learning and wellbeing of students, staff and families?

In answering this question, we should consider the following factors:
- **Workplace health and safety**: Will the action keep people safe?
- **Transparency**: Do stakeholders understand the rationale for the action?
- **Best interests of the majority**: Is the action in the best interests of the majority of stakeholders?
- **Fairness**: Does the action meet the needs of stakeholders?
- **Practicality and sustainability**: Can the action be done and continue to be done?
- **Cost-benefit analysis**: Does the cost of the action warrant the outcome?
- **Legal requirements**: Does the action meet the obligations of relevant legislation?

Each chapter presents a range of scenarios including a dilemma for leaders and teachers and options for how they might respond. These scenarios are based on my real-life experience as a school principal and illustrate how I managed a situation or how I observed others manage the situation. The options provided are not comprehensive; rather, they are offered as ideas for consideration. You may not agree with them – that's fine. Let's start the conversation.

Readers may question why relationships are so important in an industry where teaching and learning is the core business. Here is the rationale: parents cannot provide a complete education for their children without teachers, and teachers cannot provide all opportunities for their students without parents. Parents are the primary educators of their children, but for six hours per day teachers stand *in loco parentis* – in place of the parents – in educating the children. Apart from the students themselves, teachers are the most important people in a child's education at school; hence strong and positive relationships across all school stakeholders are crucial.

While this book is largely directed at school leaders and teachers, Chapter 6 discusses advice for parents on building positive relationships with other parents, which may be shared when appropriate. The examples given serve to emphasise the philosophy that teachers and parents must work together, as explored further in my first book, *Are You Ready for School?*.

Protocols are easier to follow for employees (school staff) and their clients (parents and students) when there is a transparent rationale behind them. A transparent rationale builds a culture of trust and collaboration through strengthening relationships. It almost sounds like the chicken and egg dilemma. Which comes first? Neither and both.

Chapter 1

ENROLMENTS

When a family makes an initial enquiry to enrol their child at a school, first impressions count for both the school and the family. Whether the initial communication is face-to-face or via telephone, email or social media, the response that school staff provide can make or break the relationship very quickly.

Ideally school leaders will have the five P's in place to support a consistent approach to responding to enrolment enquiries. In doing so they will be able to build positive relationships very quickly. This chapter unpacks the critical importance of balancing the five P's and building relationships with families from the moment they make an enquiry to the moment their child leaves the school. It also stresses the significance of the relationship between parents and teachers in building a culture of trust, collaboration and enquiry.

Each decision a school leader makes must be measured against the key criteria: *will it improve students' learning?* While schools are about more than just academic achievements, improving students' learning achievements is their core business. Schools may use other metrics to measure school performance and improvements, such as engagement, relationships, post-school options and curriculum offerings. So maybe the question should be: *will it improve the learning and wellbeing of students, staff and families?*

> The movie *The Blind Side*, starring Quinton Aaron and Sandra Bullock, is based on the true story of Michael Oher, an African American high school student who was adopted by a wealthy white family, Sean and Leigh Anne Tuohy. They provided him with great opportunities – more than his birth parents were able to provide.
>
> Upon achieving success in high school, Michael was scouted by many of the top universities for a football (gridiron) scholarship. To be eligible for a football scholarship Michael had to achieve academic grades that met college entrance standards. The Tuohy's employed a private tutor to assist Michael in lifting his grades. He achieved the required grades, graduated from high school and was chased by many colleges.
>
> During the selection process Michael was interrogated by the assistant director of law enforcement for the National Collegiate Athletic Association to determine whether he had been influenced by his adopted parents, who were promoting their alma mater, "Ole Miss", the University of Mississippi. The assistant director was investigating whether Michael was making an independent decision about his future. As Michael responded to the assistant director, it is perfectly normal for families to influence their children's decisions and normal for children to consider following their parent's footsteps in going to their alma mater.

As demonstrated in *The Blind Side*, opportunities for students can vary from school to school. This still applies in today's society across cities, states and countries. Families usually want what is best for their children, including a school that can best meet their educational needs. There are unique criteria for government schools, religious based schools and private schools. Such criteria can include the residential address of the family being within the catchment area of the school, the faith background of the families being aligned to the school's philosophy and the academic achievement of the student. Should families be able to 'buy' an education or bend the rules to gain entry to a school, or should enrolment criteria overrule any exceptional circumstances? Key relationships between families and staff start at the point of enrolment enquiries.

Enrolment Criteria

When there is excessive demand on enrolment places for schools, criteria for enrolment may need to be applied. Depending on the school, school leaders may employ a range of selection criteria to identify who they can enrol or, in some cases, interview to enrol. Some of the enrolment criteria school leaders may adopt are:

- catchment (geographical boundaries in suburbs around the school)
- sibling (the child is a sibling of an existing student)
- other family connection (for example, the student may be the child of a past pupil)
- financial considerations (the family can meet the financial obligations of the school).

In the case of faith-based schools, the criteria may extend to include:

- same faith as the school
- similar faith to the school
- family connections (family members of same faith as school).

These criteria are relatively self-explanatory and generally allow school leaders to follow the five P's. At this point it is important to note that enrolment criteria should be transparent and available to all prospective families. When schools fail to promote their criteria publicly it makes it very difficult for prospective families to understand why they were denied a place.

There are numerous education authorities, models of schools and governance structures, all of which make their own decisions regarding their own five P's. Schools under the same education authorities should have similar five P's, but this is not always the case – and that makes life confusing for prospective families who enrol at multiple schools with different enrolment criteria. Schools under the same education authority should have the consistent and transparent enrolment criteria. And if the education authority allows schools autonomy, then schools in close proximity who know families do "shop around" should work together on identical and transparent enrolment criteria, even including timelines for the enrolment of children for the yearly intake. It is accepted that families may enrol mid-year in schools, knowing the same enrolment criteria still applies.

For schools whose enrolment criteria may include the geographical catchment areas, school leaders have the challenge of balancing the need the needs of individual families who have personal reasons to want enrol the child in that school while living outside the catchment area.

How do principals of private schools choose one student over another when on the surface the students have similar backgrounds? Do the parents' jobs or background come into deliberations? If so, is this criteria known? Should the parents' jobs affect their child's educational opportunities at particular schools? For selective schools, the criteria may be more open to interpretation, as it is not widely publicised.

There are countless examples of families with what appears to be very similar familial profiles and backgrounds, yet one family gets offered a place for their child while the other family is denied a place in the same intake. When enrolment criteria are not transparent, parents who are denied a place can be left bemused, confused and baffled.

Siblings

Siblings are often an automatic enrolment to schools. It is quite common that siblings may not even go through an enrolment interview before being offered a place. However, there is great value in meeting every child when enrolling students, particularly at primary schools but also in high schools. Even if a child has an older brother or sister at the school, this should not preclude them from having an enrolment interview and having their profile understood by a member of the school leadership team. Every child deserves the same process as other students and school leaders, and all families should expect each child to have an enrolment interview, allowing that child to be valued as an individual. The enrolment interview gives the family an opportunity to share particular stories about that child and allows a member the leadership team to get to know that child in their own right. Allowing siblings an enrolment interview emphasises the importance of that relationship and the importance of acknowledging each child as their own person.

There will be occasions where siblings of current students may not be offered a place. This is a huge dilemma for school leaders. For example, if a sibling has significant learning needs, it may not be possible for the school to provide the educational resources necessary for them, and the principal may be unable to offer a place without further needs assessment. This situation underscores the importance of every child having an enrolment interview, whether they are a sibling or not. Siblings will more than likely be guaranteed a place if their educational needs can be met.

Financial Considerations

Most schools have some financial expectations on families. The minimum families may be expected to pay may be for just books and uniforms. The maximum families may be required to pay for their child's education may include tuition fees; levies for various school activities; a building, library and/or capital fund; fees for extracurricular activities; and accommodation in the case of boarding schools. These financial commitments range from a few hundred dollars per year to tens of thousands of dollars per year.

During the enrolment process the financial expectations on families should be explained to the family, promoting the culture of transparency. If the school has strict protocols around the financial commitments being met by the family, then families who cannot afford the school fees, levies and mandatory financial commitments may self-select and withdraw from the process. Many schools will list their school's fees and levies on their website so families may start the enrolment process with full knowledge of what is expected.

When families wish to enrol their child at a school and it is beyond their financial means or their financial circumstances change, making their family's capacity to pay the fees and levies difficult, difficult conversations need to be had between the parents and the school leaders. In some schools the principal has the discretion to enrol students knowing the parents cannot meet the financial commitment. Some schools may have finance committees that guide the protocols around enrolling students with limited financial backing. When the principal has the discretion to make decisions about enrolments, they may have to balance following the five P's and building relationships with the families.

Children with Diverse Needs

Enrolling children with diverse needs can present a challenge for leaders of mainstream schools. Families may have a personal reason to want their child to be at that school; for example, they might have children already enrolled at the school or they might want the child to have the same kind of educational experience they had. The principal and the staff may not be able to meet that child's educational and social needs in their entirety or at all. How does a principal manage balancing that relationship within the processes and protocols that the employing authority would recommend?

There are numerous variables that principals need to consider when enrolling children with significant learning needs. Firstly, they must be conscious not to discriminate against a child who has a disability. The *Disability Discrimination Act 1992* ensures that all children have a right to a high-quality education. The *Disability Standards for Education 2005* requires principals to ensure children are not discriminated against based on disability. There are numerous other pieces of legislation at the federal level to ensure that schools comply with the anti-discrimination practices, including the *Age Discrimination Act 2004, Racial Discrimination Act 1975* and *Sex Discrimination Act 1984*.

These pieces of legislation recognise that students have a range of personal characteristics and experiences, including:

+ disability
+ gifted and talented
+ gender and sexual orientation
+ out-of-home care
+ refugee or migrant background
+ culturally and linguistically diverse background
+ Aboriginal and Torres Strait Islander background
+ rural or remote families
+ mental health and wellbeing
+ marginalised and disengaged.

It is important that school leaders are confident when offering a family a place for their child with diverse needs that the student's needs can be met. The factors that principals need to consider include the capacity to provide the educational resources, both personnel and physical, to meet the student's needs. The principal should listen to the parents to understand their hopes and dreams for their child's education and then begin consultation with specialists, support teachers, members of their leadership team and the parents. The principal will then determine if it is possible for the school to meet the student's needs within the resources available to the school.

The principal will also need to consider the impact of enrolling this student on their school. While this might sound harsh, if the child's enrolment has a negative impact on the teacher's ability to fulfill their role, then it will impact not only that child's education but the education of many students. Is that fair? This is a very sensitive topic and one that can involve both risks and possibilities. Children with learning disabilities add to the rich tapestry of the school environment. Some teachers embrace the enrolment of such children with great passion and enthusiasm because they want to provide a high-quality education for all students. Other teachers are less willing to welcome students with diverse learning needs and make it difficult for a principal to enrol students. The principal may know a teacher is reluctant and will struggle and that it will become very difficult to provide a high-quality education with the reluctant teacher in front of that child. This presents a dilemma for the principal: to enrol a child knowing their education will not be high quality and will require additional support from other staff or to deny the enrolment. Teachers, in primary schools in particular, are generalists and sometimes believe they do not have the necessary skills or training to meet the needs of students with a disability. Some teachers may not have the skills, while others may have the skills but lack the confidence to trust their skills. Despite best intentions there are occasions where children with significant learning needs may be better served in educational settings other than a mainstream primary or high school.

It is imperative to also remember that the enrolment of a child with significant learning needs is not just for one year, it is for the duration of that child's education at that school. There might be provisions by which a school can review a child's enrolment, so these protocols would need to be clearly explained to families at the point of enrolment. A child's verification (the process by which a child's needs are assessed to meet the education authority's criteria, often to attract funding for additional support) may be reviewed as their needs may change as they get older; however, this may or may not have an impact on whether or not the child will continue to be enrolled to that school. When a principal offers a family a place for their child, generally speaking it is for the duration of the time that child is at school. If the child's needs change, it may be necessary to review the school's capacity to continue to meet that child's needs.

What this does is stress the importance of the relationship between parents and teachers. Open communication, open dialogue, a willingness to learn, a willingness to engage and a willingness to share stories and experiences will all go a long way to make the educational experience a positive one for the student, their family and the teacher. These protocols must be outlined very clearly at the point of enrolment so that the teacher and the parents are on the same page, have similar expectations and understand the process of education for their child. If the culture of trust, collaboration and enquiry is established early, then a positive relationship may be built quickly for the benefit of the child and teacher.

As educational leader Stephen Covey contends, we all want win-win situations for everyone (Covey 1989).

When children are being added to the Australian commonwealth census Nationally Consistent Collection of Data on School Students with Disability (NCCD) register, which collects data about students with significant learning needs in schools, there are occasions when parents can be informed about their children's inclusion on the register with minimal information. So there is a question as to whether or not teachers and school leaders should be completely transparent when sharing with parents the process, rationale and outcomes of their children being included in the NCCD database. In reality some of these children will not attract government funding. Sharing the process would provide an awareness that teachers need to make adjustments for these students. There will be some children who are imputed – that is, they do not have a diagnosis, but staff believe they have enough evidence to warrant inclusion in one of the NCCD categories – so the student will be included in the NCCD database with or without the parents' permission. If school staff are intending to build and create positive, harmonious, collaborative relationships with parents, how much should they tell the parents, particularly parents who may be reluctant to acknowledge their child has additional learning needs? Here's the balancing act.

There is another significant issue that staff need to navigate when working with the NCCD database. Should staff be expected to contribute more information with the recording of more adjustments than the minimum requirements? This creates a dilemma for Learning Support teachers working with classroom teachers in terms of balancing their professional relationships while expecting exceptionally high standards. The majority of teachers appreciate the support provided to ensure all students can access the curriculum. The NCCD process requires teachers to record adjustments made to support students. The higher the frequency of adjustments across multiple subjects, the more funding a student may attract. This funding may be used for additional staff, often teacher aides, or intervention teachers, along with resources and staff training. The NCCD process ideally should become part of good teacher practice in recording adjustments (differentiation) and reviewing the impact ("Know thy impact", Hattie 2008).

Learning Support teachers are best placed to understand the probable level of funding a child may attract based on the evidence provided. There are occasions where teachers may have made significant adjustments to accommodate a child's learning needs. However, if the adjustments are not recorded, the evidence required to attract the level of funding the child need may be missing. If the Learning Support teacher believes more evidence is required to add weight to the student's profile, they need to encourage teachers to do more while respecting their teacher's workload and effort. This may create a tension and may need careful juggling to build professional relationships across the teaching teams while following the expected processes.

For teachers who need to add to their evidence for students, they may seek time away from class to write up their adjustments. There is a matter of equity here, as other teachers may have done what is expected without time away from class. It may create a divide in the teaching staff if some teachers appear to be "rewarded" with time, support and supervision from the Learning Support team for not completing the recording of adjustments as required. There's another dilemma for school leaders to manage.

Enrolling children is one of the great joys for school principals. Meeting families who are new to a school community and hearing their stories and rationales for choosing the school brings great satisfaction to principals. Promoting their school to new families provides principals the opportunity to articulate the unique qualities of the school. Enrolling children also comes with enormous responsibility to the students, the families and the staff. A principal's goal is to provide high-quality teaching and learning for all students. Failure to do this is not an option.

Scenarios to Consider

Scenario 1

Context: A minor celebrity has moved cities and wants to enrol their children at a particular school. The celebrity has contacts in the city and is advised to name-drop during the enrolment process in the hope that the protocols may be bent to accommodate their family. A member of the school's governing board recommends that the principal bend the protocols to accommodate the celebrity's children, but the principal has already denied enrolments for families with children in the same grade levels based on enrolments being at capacity.

Dilemma: The principal is conscious that one or two children may in fact make little difference to the particular class or year level. However, they are also conscious that they have already declined some families, quoting that the classes are already full. The principal appreciates the support of the board member, who is a very influential member within the community, recommending the enrolment of this child and is reluctant to go against their wishes. But they are also conscious of having transparent processes and protocols which build faith and trust in the broader community.

Options: As a principal, it might be appealing to have high-profile personalities within the school community. The principal could simply follow the board member's advice, enrol the family and welcome the celebrity's child into the school community. However, given the excess of demand for enrolments, if exceptions are made to enrol the children of high-profile people, this is likely to raise eyebrows and diminish trust within the broader community who weren't afforded the same privilege.

Alternately the principal could revisit the numbers in the relevant year levels or classes and reassess if there is any provision for the enrolment of any other child. This is following due process and allowing the principal to reassess previous decisions without being forced or railroaded into making a pressure decision. In effect, the principal is buying some time so that they can be seen to be considering all the variables prior to making a decision which could in fact appear to be showing significant bias.

Finally, the principal could simply deny the child's enrolment on the basis they have already denied other families places due to class sizes. This of course could potentially jeopardise the relationship between the school board member and the principal. However, it may in fact strengthen that relationship, because the principal is indicating courage in their convictions and not allowing the board member to influence what is ultimately a principal's decision, not a board member's decision. Courageous, ethical principals may go against the wishes of individuals to make morally sound decisions, which shows their strength of character. It is not always easy, though, particularly when faced with pressure from influential community members. The principal's decision will also be appreciated by the community, who value the consistent implementation of the transparent process.

Scenario 2

Context: A faith-based school has an enrolment criteria that siblings of current students are automatic enrolments. One class is close to being full, with the capacity for one more child, but the school has received multiple enquiries for that place. The school leader must choose between the sibling of a current student with no faith background and a child of the same faith background as the school.

Dilemma: Should the school leader follow the enrolment criteria to the letter, or should they assess each family on their profile and the needs of the students, teachers and families? If the school was established to meet the needs of the faith community, is it reasonable and fair to deny a child of that faith a place in favour of a sibling with no faith connection but a connection to the school community? Do family connections outweigh a school's faith culture?

Options: This scenario highlights how transparent criteria will promote understanding of enrolment processes within the community. Splitting up families is rarely an option, so the sibling should be enrolled.

Denying a faith-filled family a place for their child does, however, set a huge precedent, which could send a message that faith commitment comes second to families of no faith. Hence it may be prudent to accommodate the faith-filled family as well. It is a difficult decision for the principal, especially if the classes are perceived to be full.

Alternately the principal could contact a neighbouring faith-based school to determine if that setting could an option for the family. Somehow the faith-filled family must be found a place in a faith-based setting.

Scenario 3

Context: A mother with four children, all with Autistic Spectrum Disorder (ASD), makes an enrolment enquiry at a primary school. Her ex-husband is not heavily involved in their children's upbringing, leaving her to make the decisions around their children's education. The situation requires the enrolment of four children with special needs into four different year levels. The school already has some children with disabilities in the year levels which the children would be entering.

Dilemma: The principal is conscious of the of the class profiles in the year levels these children would be entering. Two of the classes have significant existing challenges and the teachers are already working under stress. However, the two other year levels are in a position to welcome the new enrolments. Should the principal offer to enrol all four children or only two of the children, remembering that sibling enrolments are almost automatic assuming the child's education needs can be met?

Options: The principal would be advised to seek support from the relevant education authority as to what processes should be followed to ensure they act in accordance with their obligations under the *Disability Discrimination Act 1992* and the *Disability Standards for Education 2005*. The principal would also be wise to seek advice from their learning support team as to what provisions are in place to accommodate these new children.

The principal should explain the class profiles to the family so they are aware that their hopes and dreams for their children's education may not be met if enrolment was to proceed for two of the children.

The principal could consider offering enrolment places to two of the children, knowing that those children's needs can be accommodated but the needs of the other two children cannot. If the parent wishes for all of their children to be enrolled at the same school, and the principal is only in a position to offer places for two of the children, then the family has a difficult decision to make. The family could wait for the next round of enrolments, which is likely to be the following year. Transparent communication of the school's enrolment processes is important to build relationships, especially during a negotiation.

Note: this scenario is based on a true story. The principal decided to offer places to two of the children only. The family declined the enrolment until the school was in a position to offer a place to all four children, which happened one year later.

Summary

Enrolments are the initial point of contact for school staff and parents to build relationships. Within the numerous family models and various criteria for enrolment at different schools, principals need to be transparent in following the five P's so families feel there is equity in the enrolment process whether their child is offered a place or not. Families have the right to understand enrolment criteria and how they relate to the school's commitments to provide a high-quality education for all students. School leaders should use the five P's to guide their work of enrolling students so they meet their obligations. They can balance the five P's with clear and transparent communication to establish, build and maintain positive relationships within their school community.

"People need to choose humanity."

Alicia Hanham, Chaplain,
St Martin's School, Carina

Think of your own ENROLMENTS scenario and do a response analysis

Scenario:

Dilemma:

Options:

Response checklist:

- ☑ **Does the response improve the learning and wellbeing of students, staff and families?**
- ☑ **Workplace health and safety**: Will the action keep people safe?
- ☑ **Transparency**: Do stakeholders understand the rationale for the action?
- ☑ **Best interests of the majority**: Is the action in the best interests of the majority of stakeholders?
- ☑ **Fairness**: Does the action meet the needs of stakeholders?
- ☑ **Practicality and sustainability**: Can the action be done and continue to be done?
- ☑ **Cost-benefit analysis**: Does the cost of the action warrant the outcome?
- ☑ **Legal requirements**: Does the action meet the obligations of relevant legislation?

Chapter 2

STAFFING

This chapter unpacks the protocols, processes, procedures, practices and policies that are in place to support the fair and just employment of staff. It is a complex business to appoint the right people for the right job, hence the five P's are in place to support those doing the recruitment. There are many variables that employing authorities need to consider when advertising, interviewing and appointing successful candidates and, sadly, disappointing the people who missed out.

The purpose of employing teachers, teacher aides and deputies is to ensure we have the right staff to provide a high-quality education for all students. The relationships that staff create within their own professional networks are also vital to high-performing schools. So while the five P's are in place to support the employment process, the relationships created during and after the selection process are key to creating a high performing school.

Based on a true story, *Hidden Figures* highlights the injustice of segregation protocols in America in the 1960s, when African Americans were regularly discriminated against. Al Harrison was leading a team of mainly white male scientists to plan for a return space flight at NASA. The team of scientists included one black female scientist, Katherine Johnson. Johnson was a vital team member, but she was spending an extraordinary amount of time away from her desk each day. When Harrison asked where she went every day, Johnson explained that she had to travel halfway across the campus to use the segregated bathroom for black women. Harrison understood the situation was untenable and removed the discriminatory signage from the bathroom.

Johnson and her black female colleagues weren't allowed to attend a briefing meeting with the astronauts – also according to protocols – as they didn't have the security clearance. Again Harrison bent the rules and invited Johnson to attend the trajectory and launch window division meetings. It was at one of these briefings that she solved a critical equation for the astronauts that identified the landing zone of the capsule returning to earth. Johnson's solution instilled confidence in the astronauts to the extent that she was called on to approve some final figures before the astronauts took flight. Her relationship with the astronauts outweighed the protocols of the time.

Initially black female scientists weren't allowed to be supervisors or program the new IBM computer, which calculated answers necessary for the space journeys. Eventually Dorothy Vaughan, another black scientist, was promoted to supervisor and her black female mathematician colleagues were allowed to program the IBM computer. It took a strong leader to override protocols that were preventing progress to effect change.

Hidden Figures contains many parallel stories where accepted protocols of the time were initially upheld by leaders. It took a need, a desire and a willingness by some to fight for the basic human right of equality to break protocols, for relationships to be strengthened and for change to happen.

Employment Criteria

In our current world should employers discriminate on the basis of gender? Does such discrimination still exist in our world? History provides many examples where gender or race were used to set protocols and then discriminate against people because that was the expected and accepted practice. Yet some brave people valued the relationships between those being discriminated against and their employers or society and so bent or broke the protocols to build relationships. And aren't we grateful that history has evolved.

It is sad to see that there are still gender pay gaps in some professions. As recently as 10 October 2021, it was reported that Queensland's current State Police Commissioner, a woman, was employed on a significantly lower wage than her male predecessor (Lang 2021). This is stunningly bad news.

The criteria for employment of teachers and teacher aides may include the following:

- registration
- qualifications
- experience
- suitability for vacancy
- X-factor (a unique skill or quality they may offer the school community)
- cultural diversity
- skill set
- employment costs
- personal story
- longevity in role and school.

Note that these criteria are relatively general and may be applied to many other industries. Some of these protocols allow for some leader autonomy while others are mandated and must be followed. Let me make the distinction so employment criteria may be understood and followed while promoting positive relationships as much as possible.

Teacher **registration** within the accreditation body is a mandated criteria for employment within schools. There are minimal (if any) ways that these criteria can be stretched. The mandated criteria are often the easiest to use to filter applicants. If a teacher is registered in another state or jurisdiction, employment can be considered if they have the capacity to obtain registration in the local jurisdiction before employment.

For teaching positions there are minimum **qualifications** for employment. A teaching degree and qualifications at the relevant level are expected. Is there any room to employ someone outside these standards? Yes. There are numerous examples where secondary school teachers are asked to teach subjects outside their field of expertise and without specific training or qualifications in the field. This is less than ideal, yet it happens. In primary schools the qualification necessary for employment is to have a teaching degree, which could be a general degree; an early childhood degree; or a postgraduate degree. The length of these courses varies and the volume of practical experiences (practicums) varies, while the expectations for teaching in a primary school classroom are similar.

Relevant **experience** is often used as another criterion for employment. This criterion allows for great autonomy for school leaders. All teachers started as graduates as their careers began. On some occasions experience would be ideal for candidates to fulfil the vacancy. On other occasions experience may not be necessary and the school can provide the necessary support for the new teacher. There is a lot of latitude with the degree of experience school leaders may choose to deem relevant for employment of staff.

Suitability for the vacancy can include many filters for school leaders to consider and allows for a lot of latitude. Factors such as experience at the same year level; the team of teachers in or around the vacancy; willingness to fulfil obligations for that year level – for example, being able to attend camps and sporting events and lead creative opportunities such as the senior musical; and knowledge of the curriculum for the vacancy.

The **X-factor** (as I call it) is a unique quality that makes a candidate stand out from the crowd. Individuals may have a unique gift that they may be willing to share with the school community. Musical talents, athletic ability, community connections and training in a specialised field are examples of X-factors that school leaders may value when considering candidates for employment. This criteria similarly allows for a degree of latitude.

Cultural diversity is another criterion school leaders may use when splitting hairs over suitable candidates. Schools may have a cultural identity that can be strengthened by staff cultural diversity. There may be great value in employing staff with an Indigenous background, not solely because they are First Nations peoples but because they can promote important cultural nuances from a personal perspective.

Some teaching positions require teachers to have unique **skill sets**. When employing a music teacher, for example, it is essential for the teacher to have the necessary skills to fulfil the role. This criteria is similar to suitability for the role. Often specialist teachers are required to have unique skills.

If candidates are shortlisted for interviews, the panel generally believes that they can do the job, so something must make the preferred candidate stand out. The criteria described above provide some guidelines and some strict protocols.

Nowadays there is another criterion that school leaders may be reluctant to acknowledge. Let me be brave and say the **cost** of a teacher may also be a criterion used to split candidates. Schools are under ever-increasing pressure from governing bodies to work within budgetary limitations while still providing a high-quality education for all students. The cost of a very experienced teacher compared to a graduate teacher is significant, to the tune of tens of thousands of dollars. In some schools that financial difference can make a huge difference to other resources that can be provided. As one of my deputies reminded me recently, it is a sad day when teachers are employed based on how much they cost the school. This should never be the sole determining factor; however, there is no denying that it is considered in some school communities.

Wait – there's more.

When reviewing contracts for current staff, it is common for some staff to plead their case as to why they need to be employed.

- "I need this job because I have financial commitments."
- "I am a single parent and the only provider for my family."
- "I have huge financial debt including a mortgage and school fees."
- "This job gives me a sense of purpose – I would be lost without it."
- "I know I can contribute to the community and am willing to do anything."

I have heard all these **personal stories** and more from staff pleading their case. Should personal stories be a criteria for employment? This again should not be the sole determining factor, rather a filter through which the school leaders may view the candidates, if in fact they know the personal stories. This is most often possible for current contract staff who are applying for contract renewals or permanent appointments. This is about building relationships as this practice allows for great latitude and personal bias from the school leaders.

Beyond these criteria is the **length of service** at the school or with the employing authority for current contract teachers, which school leaders may wish to consider. A very experienced teacher with many years of service, assuming they are a good practitioner, appears to be good value. But conversely an inexperienced teacher may bring fresh eyes, ideas and experience and can be trained in the ways of the school, while the long serving teacher may be stuck in their ways (sometimes, not always).

The reality is that a school's staffing levels and budgets may change from year to year. School leaders are charged with working within budgets and staffing levels, and they have an obligation to manage staffing levels and budgets in a responsible way. As responsible leaders, school leaders need to adhere to the five P's. This all sounds very clinical – and to some extent it is clinical, in the sense that there are formulas and criteria school leaders can follow – but then you add the human element, the personal stories, the emotional connection and the needs and wants of fellow teachers to the choices to be made between high quality teachers.

Once school leaders have a list of possible criteria for consideration, they need to work out a process by which an informed and proper decision may be made. Do they stick with the protocols, or do they value established relationships and foster those? And how do they weight the various parts of the employment process – that is, the interview; the written application, which may address important key result areas; the referee reports; and the experience the candidates would bring to the role? Are these weighted equally or are some of these variables more important? Some panels and recruiting agencies use a numerical system to evaluate candidates before and after interviews, which keeps the process transparent and bound by the five P's.

Appointment Process

The process for appointment may start with advertising the vacancy. School leaders may have to determine how far and wide they advertise a vacancy and how long to keep applications open. Ideally school leaders want to attract the best candidates possible and appoint in the best interests of the school community.

A panel will be convened, often comprising school leaders plus some other school representatives if relevant for the appointment process; however, this may depend on the role and the school culture. Faith-based schools may invite a religious community leader to be a panel member. Parent leaders may be included if the school leaders need and want their input. Representatives of school boards or Parents and Friends associations are common panel members. Employing authorities may also have a representative available for panels if relevant. The size of the panel should be representative of the community without being overwhelming for the candidates. All panel members need to add value to the interview process. There is some latitude for school leaders in terms of the panel membership. In some cases the employing authority may prescribe the panel membership, which directs the school leaders. This is an example of the five P's in operation.

Before the interview process the panel needs to determine the relevant questions and who will be asking them. This should be consistent to be fair to the candidates and the panel. Similarly, the timing of interviews should be considered, as this can affect the performance of the candidates and the panel. Late afternoon interviews may not allow for the optimum performance from panellists or candidates. Seating arrangements for the interviews may also affect the performance of the candidates and the panellists. Seating arrangements can create an image of welcome, inclusion and collaboration. Alternately, seating plans can create an image of authority, power and position. It will be up to the school leaders and/or panel chair to create the desired environment. So far the processes, procedures, practices, protocols and policies are in full swing, with some degree of latitude for the school leaders.

To conclude the appointment process, candidates must be notified of the outcome. This process varies from panel to panel, but it is a significant opportunity to build relationships, even with unsuccessful candidates. Firstly, the successful candidate should be called or invited to a meeting to offer them the job. Once they have accepted, the unsuccessful candidates must be notified. One model is for the panel chair to call the unsuccessful interviewees and offer them feedback. In giving the unsuccessful interviewees the bad news, the delivery can either build a relationship or destroy it very quickly. It is important to remember that each candidate interviewed could in all likelihood do the job.

An honest way to deliver the bad news without making a candidate feel like a failure is to say, "We have offered the job to someone else" rather than "You were unsuccessful". At this point feedback may be offered to the candidates. Applicants who were not interviewed also need to be notified that the process has concluded. This is often done as a group email and may include best wishes for their future endeavours. It may include an offer to keep the candidate's details on file for future reference. This part of the process is sometimes overlooked as unimportant, but it is key to building relationships even while delivering disappointing news to those candidates who didn't get a position.

When candidates receive feedback, this too can build relationships if the feedback is honest, meaningful and relevant. The challenge for the panel is they are often splitting hairs over high-quality candidates. For the candidate who came a close second or third, it may not be a case of the person not being suitable, skilled or qualified. It may be case that the community was looking for someone with very specific qualities. It may not be an issue of who is better, rather it may be that the successful candidate will bring different qualities to the community. It is never an easy message to hear or deliver, but if done well it can build relationships for future possibilities.

While the details for the process for legitimate vacancies – that is, those where there are no preferred candidates prior to the appointment process – may vary from the details for vacancies where there are preferred or known candidates, the outcome should be the same: high-quality teachers who provide a high-quality education for all students.

It does get interesting when interviewees are a mix of known and preferred candidates and unknown candidates. The panel must now rely on the five P's for consistency and transparency. This is a huge challenge when panel members will automatically bring personal bias to the conversation. Unconscious bias exists in all walks of life and employment. Panellists must be aware of this and manage it appropriately so the five P's are maintained while building relationships.

Teacher appointments can be very emotive and sometimes divisive. Colleagues will have an opinion and may even express it (not always a wise thing to do). Parents too will have opinions, especially if the appointment impacts on their children. Teachers need to be supportive of all their colleagues, not divisive. And parents need to trust the process of teacher appointment as their experience is limited to their interactions with the teachers, often through their children.

This can be a difficult area to navigate for school leaders.

Allocating Teachers to Year Levels

Some of the most passionate debates school leaders have on an annual basis is the allocation of teachers to year levels and teaching teams in preparation for the following year. Principals have to manage different staffing models which are in the best interests of the students and the entire staff, while also considering individual teachers' needs, wishes and priorities.

Every teacher has their own unique style when in front of a class. There may be similarities across some colleagues, while others may have great variety, even within teaching teams (teachers on the same year level or within the same faculty). Ideally school leaders try to create teaching teams that are cohesive, collaborative, harmonious and positive (feel free to add your own descriptors here). When school leaders have the annual conversation about assigning teachers to year levels, they have various factors to consider. Here are some considerations school leaders may discuss:

1. Consistent model of teaching (open-plan teaching model, composite and multi-age models)
2. The teaching teams' disposition (friends'/colleagues' philosophy)
3. Experience within the teaching team (Are there strong leaders?)
4. Diversity within the team
5. Experience from the previous year (Do they know the year level expectations?)

Of course, these considerations are possible where there are multiple classes per year level and/or faculty. Where there is a single-stream school, it makes it somewhat more challenging to build cohesive teams across year levels when teachers may feel isolated in their year level.

How does a principal determine which staff are most appropriate to keep when they have high-quality staff but a limited number of vacancies? Does the principal work on the principle of loyalty to existing staff, do they work on staff with particular skill sets, or do they work on staff with particular cultural advantages? For example, Aboriginal and Torres Strait Islander teachers may bring particular skills that the school needs. Does the principal work on which teacher's appointment would cost the least if they have limited finances? Or do they fill the vacancy with the teacher most suited to the position based on qualifications and experience? These are all dilemmas that principals have to balance when working within protocols while trying to maintain relationships with and within their staff.

Performance Management

Sometimes teaching teams do not gel. Sometimes teaching teams become dysfunctional and toxic. As disappointing as it is to acknowledge this possibility, they do exist and need to be managed. School leaders on occasions must place teachers where they will do the least damage within a team and for the students. Some people may ask why these teachers still have positions working with students. The sad reality is that is very difficult to move a teacher on and far more difficult if the teacher has not been given feedback about their work or their professional relationships.

Brené Brown is an American research professor who is considered an expert in the fields of courage, vulnerability, shame and empathy. She explains the conditions under which people may value feedback:

> *"If you're not in the arena also getting your ass kicked, I'm not interested in your feedback. If you have constructive feedback you want to give me, I want it ... But if you're in the cheap seats, not putting yourself on the line, and just talking about how I can do it better, I'm in no way interested in your feedback."* (Brown, 2020)

All staff deserve feedback to affirm and improve their practice. School leaders should give staff regular and timely feedback. For the feedback to be meaningful, it must be relevant and shared in a timely manner.

In the event that a staff member requires feedback of a serious nature which leads to disciplinary action, the lowest level of intervention from the school leader is the preferable place to start. The lowest level usually involves the school leaders discussing the alleged incident and seeking the staff member's account of the incident. The school leader can then share the relevant policies and protocols that they may be breaching. Disciplining staff at the lowest level builds relationships within the procedures and practices.

Should the disciplinary actions be of greater magnitude then stricter protocols will be followed. The higher the level of investigation the more rigorous the processes must become. Education authorities have robust processes they follow when disciplining staff. On these occasions the five P's outweigh the relationships that exist between employers and employees, and it is important that the five P's are followed in a transparent manner.

Dress Codes

Shahar Erez, Co-Founder and CEO at Stoke Talent in Sunnyvale, California shared an example of how a person's appearance may influence their opportunities for employment (2021). A man refused to turn on his camera during Zoom interviews. Purely using his voice and experience he had won various jobs. Once he saw the candidate in person, however, Erez understood his reluctance to be seen. The applicant was covered in tattoos and had previously experienced discrimination and prejudice from people reacting negatively to his appearance. This begs the question: should employers be influenced by a person's appearance when determining their suitability for a position? If someone is employed sight unseen, can the employer change their mind, change the staff dress code or set unique expectations for the individual?

There are various dress codes for educational settings. What is accepted in some settings will not be accepted in others. Imagine a principal appoints a teacher who was "dressed up" for the interview, yet when the teacher appears dressed for work their tattoos are highly visible. The teacher meets the dress code, yet the principal, some colleagues and some parents may express their concern as to the suitability of this teacher's appearance. Can the principal change the staff dress code? Should the principal and community accept the teacher's appearance, knowing they are the best candidate for the position? Now, there's a balancing act. How would the principal maintain the high standards of the school while building a relationship with a new teacher who is covered in ink?

> In mid-2021 I went to the barber for my regular visit. The barber, Jacob Lihou, who provided the service was covered in ink, with full sleeve tattoos. As we were chatting, we discovered that we went to the same high school, although some 30 years apart. Jacob shared with me his passion and talent for music and relayed a story of when he was invited back to the school as a guest judge for a music competition. On receiving the invitation, he was asked to wear a long-sleeved shirt to hide his ink. Jacob happily obliged as he didn't want to display what some may consider a negative appearance to impressionable young men. Though he was a most polite and engaging barber, people may have judged him on his physical appearance. Not only was Jacob an outstanding musician, an excellent barber and good communicator, he was an excellent role model, with or without his ink.

Some schools have very explicit dress codes for their staff, and these guidelines may include the visibility and presence of piercings and tattoos. School leaders will be placing their values, and possibly the accepted and expected values of their school community, on staff, families and students. Such schools would anticipate that their staff will uphold the values by following the dress codes without question. Hence it may be unlikely that people will apply for positions in such schools if they know that their appearance may be contrary to the school standards. Imagine if during the shortlisting process, which may be done through reading applications and talking to referees with minimal or no visual access to the applicants, one or more applicants proves to have piercing or tattoos that do not align with the school guidelines. Imagine the best candidate for a position has an appearance that is at odds with the school's standards. School leaders would face an interesting decision if they were to deny someone a job over their appearance, especially if the teacher is the best candidate based on all other criteria.

Scenarios to Consider

Scenario 1

Context: An experienced, highly regarded teacher is told that her hours may be cut due to a decline in enrolments and a tightening of the school budget from which her role is funded. Upon hearing this news, the teacher asks the principal if he values her role. She also tells the principal of her personal financial commitments and her need for the hours of her role to be maintained so she can meet her personal financial obligations.

Dilemma: The principal wishes to keep the teacher while working within the limitations that have largely been imposed by the employing authority. There are also other staff facing a reduction in hours, so the principal may have to prioritise where the school should invest in their staff. Who should be selected for reduced hours and how should this be decided?

Options: Discussion with the leadership team is the first course of action, so they understand the dilemma and can possibly add to the background context of the teacher and the role. A clear rationale for the teacher and all staff allows for transparency and therefore understanding. "I wouldn't want your job" is common feedback during these conversations – welcome to leadership!

It would also be wise to share information as early as possible so the teacher has time to digest the reality and consider their options. It will also allow them time to think through the reality without an immediate emotional response. A decision in the best interests of the whole school, with an awareness of the teacher's personal needs and wants, is possible. As time evolves, other opportunities may be explored for the teacher.

Scenario 2

Context: A principal has a teacher on contract and in line for another contract the following year. As the principal is beginning to consider their options for contract appointments for next year, the teacher tells the principal that she is pregnant and will only be available for the first term. Thinking of how best to minimise interruptions for the students, it would appear sensible to not offer the teacher the contract, knowing she can't fulfil the contract term. The plan would be to appoint a teacher who can fulfil the full-year contract.

Dilemma: Can the principal discriminate and not appoint a preferred candidate when the principal knows she can't fulfil the contract because she is pregnant? Should (and can) the principal act in the best interests of the students and appoint a teacher who can teach the full year? Or should the principal appoint the teacher as the preferred candidate and manage her leave when necessary, appointing another teacher for the remainder of the year? How does the principal build relationships with the teacher, do what's best for the students (and parents), and follow the employment entitlements of the employee?

Options: Principals have to be very careful to follow the industrial legislation which reflects the employment conditions of teachers, so checking the leave conditions for expectant employees with the employing authority is important. School leaders will need to balance building the relationship with the employee and doing what is in the best interests of the students, while honouring the protocols around leave entitlements and employment conditions for pregnant staff.

Principals would also be advised to discuss the upcoming position with the expectant teacher. There could be a variety of responses from the teacher. They may not wish to accept the appointment, knowing it would disrupt the educational flow for the students. The teacher may also feel it is in their best interests not to work during this time.

If appointment of the expectant teacher is required by their employment conditions, there may be another teaching role that teacher could fill until they are ready to take maternity leave. This option would allow another teacher to work for the full contract term and provide a consistent education for the students. It may, however, cost the school more money, as the expectant teacher and the new appointee would effectively be filling one position for the duration of the expectant teacher's role before she takes leave.

Scenario 3

Context: A group of teachers, who ordinarily work as a team of three or four, are attending a professional development session where they would ordinarily sit together. Two of the team arrive early and sit at a particular table, leaving room for their colleagues. The other two team members arrive shortly afterwards and choose to sit at a different table close by, knowing that there were seats available at their colleagues' table. The first two teachers are acutely aware that they have been snubbed by their team members and are conscious of how this may look to their peers attending the same professional learning. The principal has become aware of the dysfunctional nature of this team's relationship and is working hard to create harmonious teams that are productive and collaborative within a culture of trust. This team is struggling to form those relationships, resulting in such behaviour. The principal knows that other members of the leadership team have addressed some of the disharmony and are putting in place structures that will hopefully improve the working relationship.

Dilemma: Does the principal intervene and give feedback to the staff members who chose to snub their colleagues, or do they simply allow that relationship to unfold, knowing that other members of the leadership team are working towards addressing the team dynamic?

Options: As the principal was informed of the behaviour, it would be preferable that they discuss the situation with their leadership team to understand the current strategies in place to improve that dysfunctional relationship. If there has been some improvement, then the seating arrangements witnessed may not be addressed so the principal is not seen to be micromanaging the team's behaviour.

If, however, the leadership team believes there has been no improvement in the team's collaboration, then it may be worth the principal pointing out to the second two teachers what it looked like from an outsider's point of view when they intentionally chose to sit apart from their colleagues. People do need to be aware of their behaviour in the presence of others and how their behaviour may appear to their colleagues.

While some colleagues may not have thought anything of it, others may have been observing the dysfunctional nature of the team when some choose to sit apart. It would certainly raise questions as to whether or not that team can continue in the years ahead as a teaching team. It may be necessary for the school leaders to provide mediation among the team members, especially if there is the likelihood that they will continue to work together. Regular monitoring of their cooperation and collaboration would be advisable to support the team's cohesive development. If the relationship is unworkable, then performance management may be necessary.

Summary

School leaders want the best staff doing the best job to create a high-performing schools. Every staff member brings their own strengths to the school and their own areas for growth. When employing staff, school leaders should follow the five P's of their jurisdiction, which will provide consistency and build confidence within the staff and school community. Through such confidence, positive and harmonious relationships are built. Open, honest and transparent communication is a key element in creating successful teams of people, and successful teams of school leaders, teachers and support staff are important parts of high-performing schools. Collaboration, cooperation and consultation are characteristics that typify the five P's of staffing.

"We need leaders who believe in the goodness of individuals and communities and so build cooperation and respect."

Reverend Bill Crews,
Twelve Rules for Living a Better Life

Think of your own STAFFING scenario and do a response analysis

Scenario:

Dilemma:

Options:

Response checklist:
- ☑ **Does the response improve the learning and wellbeing of students, staff and families?**
- ☑ **Workplace health and safety**: Will the action keep people safe?
- ☑ **Transparency**: Do stakeholders understand the rationale for the action?
- ☑ **Best interests of the majority**: Is the action in the best interests of the majority of stakeholders?
- ☑ **Fairness**: Does the action meet the needs of stakeholders?
- ☑ **Practicality and sustainability**: Can the action be done and continue to be done?
- ☑ **Cost-benefit analysis**: Does the cost of the action warrant the outcome?
- ☑ **Legal requirements**: Does the action meet the obligations of relevant legislation?

Chapter 3
BUDGETARY CONSTRAINTS

In a school environment money is a blessing and a curse. Too much money and school leaders have to determine how to juggle their priorities. Not enough money and school leaders are faced with potential resourcing and staffing cutbacks. The five P's are very important in guiding a principal's budgetary decision-making processes. However, building relationships is also key to creating a high-performing school. This chapter unpacks how school leaders need to balance the responsible fiscal management of a school with building positive relationships.

In the movie *Mr Holland's Opus*, starring Richard Dreyfuss, high school music teacher Glenn Holland was working on writing his own music while adjusting to family life with his wife and profoundly deaf son. In his school, the high school music program was competing for school funds along with other subject areas.

Holland was trying to build the music program so that students had similar access to music as they did to other subjects, such as sport. The school leadership had to rationalise funding allocations with limited resources. Should the sports program and music program receive similar funding? What will the rationale be for allocating more to one subject than the other? Should Holland spend more time dedicated to his music?

Holland taught in the same school for many years and upon his retirement a selection of his past pupils returned and played a piece of his music under his guidance. The concert was a great tribute to Holland, who had achieved two of his life-time goals: to lift the profile of the music program and to have a piece of his music played in public before an adoring audience. It provided personal and professional satisfaction for Mr Holland.

An underlying theme of this movie highlights that schools have competing priorities for a limited financial bucket. School leaders have to rationalise decisions to distribute funds according to school priorities. There will be many measures of accountability in place so that school leaders can be transparent in their decision-making process. Schools are accountable to their stakeholders, their education authority, the tax office and their students in providing a high-quality education. Balancing these competing priorities is not easy, especially when each school principal may have their own agenda and priorities.

Financial limitations are a reality for many schools. There is usually a finite bucket of money to provide personnel and physical resources. Decisions on how best to use these funds often present a moral dilemma for school leaders. There are always competing values within the school community, within the staff and possibly within leadership team.

Classroom Budgets

The purchasing policies of schools are often guided by very strict protocols. When teachers need to purchase resources spontaneously, by virtue of shopping, they may in fact stretch or break protocols. However, they may believe they are acting in the best interest of the needs of their students by purchasing resources economically. How do principals manage the need for a teacher to buy their own resources outside of purchasing protocols?

Staff have to work within budgets when planning for spending on consumables, copying and excursions. School leaders would be well served by telling teachers what budgets they have autonomy to manage; for example, their class consumables such as paint, glue, stickers and celebratory hospitality. If teachers are told their class budgets, they can plan effectively with full knowledge of their financial limits. (Parents shouldn't be expected to keep funding school activities.) Consumables need to add value to the curriculum activities, with rare activities undertaken purely for fun. Some primary school teachers like displaying the students' work in a "pretty" way, which often costs money. Teachers need to be discerning in their expenditure and prioritise spending that adds value to the curriculum. Making work look pretty through colourful copied cover sheets may not be the best use of discretionary funds. Teachers need to be told these parameters before they undertake what may be seen as extravagant spending. And when teachers do overspend – and some will – how should school leaders remind them of the value of the dollar? Explicit instructions, clear expectations and transparency is important for teachers and school leaders.

Similarly, teachers should have the opportunity to manage their photocopying budget if they are given an allocation for printing and paper costs. Teachers need to minimise consumable usage for financial and environmental reasons. It is common for teachers to copy pages with little more than boxes for students to complete, or a border to frame the page. Worksheets for many subjects are often copied, completed and stuck in workbooks. Could these sheets be substituted by copying off the whiteboard, or done on a device? Teachers need to reflect on their copying practices before duplicating page after page after page. Teachers should ask themselves: is there an alternative to copying that will still provide the students with the same or better outcomes? If the answer is yes, then teachers must be encouraged to find alternate models to copying.

When teachers exhaust their copying budget and come and ask school leaders to extend their budget, how should leaders respond? School leaders need to monitor teachers' copying habits and provide regular feedback. Figures don't lie. When the copying figures can be analysed to reflect the amount of paper that is used per student per week, it can reveal the model of teaching and the volume of paper being used. Once teachers know the expectations about copying, feedback can be meaningful and relevant. Explicit instructions, clear expectations and transparency is important for teachers and school leaders.

Having strict budgetary processes is important to protect families from unnecessary excessive spending and the staff from making unwise decisions without consideration for family financial circumstances. If a teacher plans an excursion for their students that is loosely associated with the curriculum, they can charge the families whatever is necessary to cover the cost of the excursion. This can seem inequitable to other teachers who spend far less and within the designated budget. Hence having strict budgetary processes are important to safeguard of spending and imposing unrealistic financial burdens on families.

If a teacher has not followed the processes, practices, protocols, procedures and policies as expected, then the school leader can easily seek further work from them before considering the excursion in its entirety. If all the paperwork is in place and the five P's have been followed by the teacher then the school leader needs to do a cost analysis to determine if this is a reasonable expense to be imposing on families if it has not already been budgeted for through an earlier levy. This is an example of where transparency and communication are key to ensure school leaders are kept informed of plans, therefore not disappointing students if excursions are declined or denied. Communication and transparency are two of teachers' greatest allies when working with not only students but also the leaders of the school, who are required to approve and support such endeavours.

Debt Collection

Chasing families for outstanding school debt is one of the least palatable jobs a school principal has to undertake. A school may have a business manager or finance secretary, who are the first people to chase families for outstanding debt, but ultimately it will come to the principal to approve the process and even to engage with families to recoup outstanding monies. After numerous attempts have been made to recover outstanding debt from families, sometimes school leaders may resort to employing debt collectors, though they know this is likely to harm any relationship between the principal and the family.

There are various communication strategies finance secretaries and business managers can apply to build relationships with families while asking them to follow the practice that is expected within their school communities. An initial phone call will build a relationship by having a conversation. This conversation may not be easy when you are talking to families about their inability to meet their financial commitments. Formalising a record of those conversations is often done through an email which confirms any agreement made during the phone conversation. When something is documented through email or formal letters it also adds a degree of formality to the process. Once again, the principal is probably going to sign those letters or at least approve them, even if it comes from a business manager or finance secretary.

Ultimately, if a school wishes to recoup outstanding monies and families are reluctant to engage in the process, school leaders can engage debt collectors to try to recover outstanding money. This is a sure way to follow process. It is also a sure way also to jeopardise relationships which may already be tenuous or may already have fallen over. Certainly engaging external people to chase families who fail to meet their financial commitments is highly likely to harm any relationship. Therefore it is important to build relationships with families at the point of enrolment and for them to understand their financial commitments. Failure to meet this commitment may result in relationships being strained if they are not forthcoming with honest information regarding their inability to meet their debt.

Should principals send debt collectors to chase families with outstanding fees with a consistent process, or is there some latitude when school leaders know the personal circumstances of families? Should principals wait until families leave the school to chase debt so the relationship isn't harmed, or should debt be chased when it reaches a limit, regardless of whether the family is still at school or not? How do school leaders approach families with the least debt above an arbitrary threshold to chase outstanding debt? And what is a reasonable timeframe to follow in the debt-recovery process? These are dilemmas that principals wrestle with regularly. Schools may have clear processes in place, and principals may rarely deviate from the process.

Governance

School leaders are well served by supportive governance structures. These structures may vary depending on which model of education authority the school operates under. Government schools are under the jurisdiction of the state education authority, and their principals may have day-to-day, week-to-week authority within the protocols of the education authority. Similarly, with faith-based schools the principal may have day-to-day, week-to-week operational authority with the added layer of religious leaders (for example, parish priests or ministers) having some authority. There may also be a school board, parish council and parish finance council that can have some authority over "their" school. This influence is slowly diminishing, yet it still exists in some communities across Australia. An independent school may have a principal for the day-to-day, week-to-week operational authority while a school board may have governance of the school's vision, staffing and budgets.

Governance structures can be a blessing and a curse. As long as the principal has the independent financial responsibility for the operations at the school, then the governing bodies should be there in an advisory capacity. This presents huge responsibilities for the principal, who in effect could be running a multimillion-dollar business, in providing a high-quality education for all their students. The principal needs that autonomy so that they can operate with a degree of flexibility within the protocols described in any employment agreement. If a principal is hamstrung by too much bureaucracy by any governing structure, it may inhibit their ability to discharge their duties to create a high-performing school.

There need to be clear parameters for any governing structure regarding the financial management of the school. There also need to be clear expectations and protocols for the principal to ensure that they are fulfilling their financial obligations responsibly. In some cases principals have to seek financial approvals for very minor expenses. This makes leading a community very challenging. Principals should value the support of governance structures that allow them the latitude to lead the school and manage the finances is in a fiscally responsible way. Any bureaucracy which jeopardises their ability to lead and run the school is contrary to the purpose of a high-quality education. Schools can't function without an income.

Educational author and speaker Adam Voigt describes the disconnect that is threatening education:

"The Venn diagram of voices who are heard when big decisions
are made about schools and the voices of actual educators
is now two circles drawn miles apart. Education policy
is now something that 'just happens' to educators. Where
does this leave us, as a state and country? We now face a
pending national teacher and principal shortage, the likes
of which we've never seen. Schools that have been hard to
staff in the past will become impossible and the very students
who most need a decent education will be denied it.
Educators beware!" (Voigt 2021)

Capital Investments

Building projects are one of the most significant capital investments schools can make. New schools are usually closely managed to be finished on time and on budget. Older schools that require capital investments for upgrading of facilities, as well as further development for growth and expansion, also require wise fiscal management. These projects are a great example of how relationships need to managed within the strict protocols associated with building projects.

Protocols for major capital investments come from a variety of sources, including any government that contributed towards the project, the governing education authority and the state education body that sets the guidelines for such project. There are obviously relationships to be managed with all the relevant stakeholders in play, including staff, the employing authority and parent associations (who may have contributed funds towards the project). Then the practical relationships between the many groups associated with the completion of the project need to be managed so the outcome meets the desired brief. Architects, builders, subcontractors, engineers, site managers and all the tradies with different skill sets and expertise, need to work in a harmonious and productive relationships within protocols. Now, how much school leaders engage with these various groups may depend on their expertise, governance structure, priorities and availability. Regardless, whether it is the school leaders or representatives from their education authority who oversee the major capital project, school leaders must have a common vision for the project to improve the quality of learning and the wellbeing of students, staff and families.

When it comes to balancing the books and keeping the project within budget, school leaders must know the school's priorities, so that if or when the budget gets stretched with variations and a developing vision, they can restructure the project to keep the priorities. The learning and wellbeing of students, staff and families should be the drivers for school improvement. It sounds simple, and in theory it could be simple, but in reality it may be different. What happens when there are competing priorities among the school leaders, staff and families?

School leaders are charged with the responsibility to ensure the prudent management of school funds. There are numerous protocols to follow and precedents set by previous leaders. Yet school leaders still wish to build relationships with their clients, the parents who entrust their children's education to their staff, and their employees, the staff responsible for providing high-quality teaching and learning, all within a budget.

Scenarios to Consider

Scenario 1

Context: Some teachers have asked their classes to plan an excursion as a class activity. As part of the maths curriculum the students are asked to identify where they would like to go an excursion, plan it, including all the associated costs and preparing a proposal to their teachers. The teachers have set a budgetary limit for the students to work within. Ultimately the school leaders will have to approve such an excursion. The teacher comes to the school leaders for approval of the same excursion.

Dilemma: The school leader needs to consider the financial burden that the teachers are imposing on the parents. If the school leaders are not familiar with the activity or the budget, how do they decide to approve the excursion when a lot of hard work and time has been invested by the students? The financial costs may be more than what the school believes is reasonable.

Options: The school leaders can read the full excursion proposal. This should include the curriculum rationale for the excursion, the financial data required to understand the excursion and a full risk assessment for the excursion. These are all necessary before the school leader can make the decision, assuming all the paperwork is in place, well in advance of the excursion date. School leaders will then need to determine whether this excursion is a worthwhile activity and will add to the high-quality teaching and learning process.

Scenario 2

Context: An old school is being funded through a new resourcing model from the government. The result is a decrease in funding for staffing. This has resulted in the school leaders proposing a school structure with large class sizes. The parents are displeased with the proposal to increase school fees and decrease staffing. It gets more complicated. The school has some reserve funds and the school leaders have identified that the school needs some physical improvements, especially around the administration building and staffroom.

Dilemma: The school leaders identify that the school facilities need an upgrade, while having to balance the needs of the students and the emotions of the families within new funding models. Should the school leaders choose the redevelopment of staff facilities while accepting large class sizes?

Options: School leaders need to explain to the community the various funding sources available to the school for the specific priorities. While the school reserve funds may be used for projects at the principal's discretion with the support of the school board and/or governing structure, the principal must have a clear rationale for directing funds in one direction.

If the school has the capacity to achieve improved staffing levels and the capital project, then it's a win-win. If the school is risking setting a precedent in keeping staffing levels higher than recommended by their education authority, then it may be time to work within staffing levels and wear the pain of large class sizes for a couple of years. This may allow the capital project to be undertaken, as long as the community is made aware of the rationale and discernment process. Once again, transparency is a school leader's friend!

Summary

Responsible stewardship of resources is a legal and moral obligation of school teachers and leaders. Being compassionate to families with financial hardship is a choice school leaders make when responding to parents in need. Schools have finite resources, so the five P's are in place to support the decisions teachers and principals may make to fulfil their roles and allow them to provide high-quality teaching within a well-resourced environment. There are occasions when school leaders and teachers have to balance the responsible allocation of funds across the school community while responding to the needs of parents and teachers and working within financial limitations.

"It is important that all staff follow protocols so that schools can meet their legal obligations."

Kylie Anderson,
Assistant Principal Administration,
St Martin's School, Carina

Think of your own BUDGETARY CONSTRAINTS scenario and do a response analysis

Scenario:

Dilemma:

Options:

Response checklist:
- ☑ **Does the response improve the learning and wellbeing of students, staff and families?**
- ☑ **Workplace health and safety**: Will the action keep people safe?
- ☑ **Transparency**: Do stakeholders understand the rationale for the action?
- ☑ **Best interests of the majority**: Is the action in the best interests of the majority of stakeholders?
- ☑ **Fairness**: Does the action meet the needs of stakeholders?
- ☑ **Practicality and sustainability**: Can the action be done and continue to be done?
- ☑ **Cost-benefit analysis**: Does the cost of the action warrant the outcome?
- ☑ **Legal requirements**: Does the action meet the obligations of relevant legislation?

Chapter 4

COMMUNICATION

Communication, both verbal and non-verbal, can build relationships very quickly and tear down relationships very quickly. School communities are microcosms of society where many people interact every day. How people treat each other will reflect the school leadership, the culture of the school and hence the quality of education being provided. Communication across schools involves staff, parents and external community members. To build a culture of trust, collaboration and enquiry it is often necessary for schools to have communication protocols in place. It is also necessary to understand that human relationships are key to building a cultural trust, collaboration, enquiry and hence high-performing schools. This chapter unpacks how we can establish those positive relationships within such protocols.

In the movie *A Few Good Men*, starring Tom Cruise, Jack Nicholson and Demi Moore, two marines, Lance Corporal Harold "Hal" Dawson and Private Louden Downey, are charged with conduct unbecoming a United States Marine when their behaviour causes the death of a fellow marine, William Santiago. During the subsequent trial they are found guilty.

Private Downey doesn't understand why they were found guilty, saying, "Hal, Hal, we did nothing wrong – we were just following orders". Lance Corporal Dawson replies, "Yes, we did something wrong. We hurt someone whom we should have been defending. We hurt Willy when we should have said no". They chose to follow their commanding officer's orders instead of acting in a morally responsible way – an example of putting protocols before relationships.

In an attempt to defend his marines, Colonel Jessup says that no marine would have disobeyed his orders not to touch Santiago. A lawyer asks why Sanitago was sent off the base if his fellow marines were ordered not to touch him. Jessup answers, "He may have been in grave danger", which was his downfall. He contradicted himself by originally saying that no-one questions his orders, yet he lied when it was suggested he had Santiago moved off the base in case someone took matters into their own hands. When pushed by the lawyer, Jessup admitted he ordered the Code Red (in-house disciplinary action on marines by other marines for poor performance). He had contradicted his own communication expectations, which resulted in him being charged.

According to Colonel Jessup no-one should question the message communicated, no-one has the latitude to think for themselves and act outside instructions and no-one has the independence to act in a morally responsible way. However, the characters had the choice to follow accepted practices or think for themselves and act in a morally responsible way. The communication between various characters in the movie all relied on open, honest and transparent communication. When the communication was vague and open to interpretation, the relationships broke down. Refined and clear communication could have resulted in a different outcome.

The communication that exists within school communities is vast and necessary. Examples of communication between key stakeholders within school communities include communication between staff members, communication between various role holders within the staff and students, communication among parents, communication between the school and families. and communication between students. How each of these stakeholders communicates with other people is essential to successful relationships.

How do parents communicate with their child's teacher? How do parents communicate with the leadership team, the secretary or staff of a school? How do parents communicate with other parents within a school setting? How do teachers communicate with their colleagues? All these communication links may work within deemed appropriate protocols as set by a school board or leadership team. However, it is critical that people within a school community maintain positive, productive relationships so that parents and teachers can work together for the benefit of the students. There are occasions where those communication protocols may be jeopardised. So how do principals, teachers and secretaries of schools navigate and build positive relationships with parents and each other while still maintaining appropriate boundaries within relevant protocols?

To ensure the communication is treated with respect, fairness and understanding it is quite common that schools put in place protocols that will give guidelines and expectations to all members of the school community. In theory it may be enough to say that all communication should be conducted in a manner of respect. There may be guidelines as to when communication can happen between staff and families. For example, is it realistic or reasonable to expect that a staff member will respond to a parent's email after 8.00 p.m.? Is it reasonable to expect that a staff member will respond to a parent's email within 24–48 hours of receiving that communication? Is it reasonable to expect that the communication should be done in the most personal and effective forum – that is, face-to-face or by telephone, not necessarily via email or letter, which allows people to be keyboard warriors? What I mean by keyboard warriors is when someone feels it quite appropriate to send what may be considered a rude and impolite message via email. These are some of the complexities when establishing communication protocols within schools. Having said that, communication is also possibly the most effective way to build relationships within school communities – hence the balancing act.

In this chapter we'll analyse each type of school relationship and the communication protocols necessary to build positive relationships that allow each member of the community the respect they are entitled to and that they deserve. The staff-to-parent relationship is one of the most common communication channels that exists in schools among adults. It is also potentially the most volatile if not handled respectfully. Hence it is important that schools do establish reasonable communication protocols when staff are communicating with parents and when parents are communicating with staff. We do not need to over-complicate things, yet we do need to have some guidelines in place.

Communicating with Parents

It is necessary to understand the media for communicating that are available to families and to staff members. Obviously face-to-face and telephone calls allow for conversations. The advantage of face-to-face is that people can see all the non-verbal expressions that go with verbal communication. Remembering that approximately 93% of a message is communicated through nonverbal communication with only 7% of the message conveyed through the spoken word, face-to-face communication is far more effective in illustrating a message than telephone calls and much preferable over letters or emails (University of Texas, n.d.).

When establishing communication protocols it is important we understand that teachers are busy people and parents are busy people. Is it reasonable to expect that a parent can turn up on the principal's doorstep or the teacher's doorstep and expect 10, 15 or 20 minutes of their time? In short, no. It would be reasonable and sustainable if the first protocol around communication is that parents make an appointment to see any member of staff, unless it is an emergency or unless it will only take less than a minute to communicate an important message. When a parent does turn up at the principal's doorstep, or the teacher's doorstep, it is up to the principal or the teacher to determine if they are in the right headspace and have the time to listen initially, and respond if possible, to the parent's issues. As a principal it may be quite acceptable for parents to appear unexpectedly and request a meeting immediately. Parents need to understand that the principal may not have time without an appointment. Similarly, parents should pay teachers the courtesy of making appointments, as teaching commitments make spontaneous conversations almost impossible during teaching time.

When a parent makes an appointment to see the principal or a staff member, the principal or staff member should ask the parent what topics they wish to raise before the engagement. This allows the principal, deputy or teacher to be prepared for the conversation. If a parent comes in and is somewhat stressed or hostile, the principal or staff member may be blindsided and put in a difficult position to respond rationally or reasonably under pressure.

School leaders should consider introducing protocols that make parents aware of communication agendas. It is quite acceptable for the principal at the start of the face-to-face meeting to set a time frame, to explain to the parent that they have allocated 10 minutes, half an hour or an hour, which they can only determine by knowing what is on the agenda. If it is a spontaneous conversation, that is far more difficult. If, however, the principal has a full diary, they can quite comfortably say to the parent, "I can give you this amount of time", which allows the parent to understand the degree of urgency with which they will need to speak and to spontaneously prepare if possible.

If, however, the parent appears on a principal's doorstep in an emergency and the principal appreciates and understands that they need to dedicate time to this parent and their particular topic of importance, then the principal may be in a position to ask their admin support to cancel or hold all other meetings and appointments until the matter is resolved. This happens on occasions for principals. It probably happens in many schools many times during the week. Here's one such example.

As an experienced principal I was once called from an assembly by my school secretary because a parent was in my office and needed to speak to me immediately. My secretary had made the judgement call upon hearing than news that this parent's child had a serious medical condition and that I needed to hear their update as soon as possible. The secretary was right in in calling me from the assembly to listen to the parent. The child had suffered a brain aneurysm and was in a critical condition in hospital, and the parent needed to update me as soon as possible. This is an example of when a principal should cancel other appointments and not necessarily give that parent a time frame. Rather, it was a time to build relationships, to be compassionate, to listen and to offer support for a family in crisis. This is an example where protocols go out the window to build relationships. And while these situations hopefully are rare, in reality they exist, and school staff need to know what to do when faced with them.

Classroom teachers don't always have the luxury to be able to teach and listen to parents at the same time. If there is capacity for staff to share responsibilities for classes when there is a crisis that teachers need to address immediately with parents, then ideally children can still be supervised and even taught while teachers meet with parents. Again, this may not be the preferred method or the preferred timing, but occasionally it does happen. It is far more preferable when possible for parents and teachers to make appointments with an agenda and time frame so they can work together in building relationships and creating a culture of trust and collaboration.

In summary, the protocols school leaders should expect of parents are:

- Parents and teachers will make an appointment to speak with each other.
- Parents and teachers will ideally tell each other the purpose of their visit (agenda).
- The school staff will set the time frame.

Questions to Lead the Conversation

The five main reasons parents engage with their children's school are:

1. to seek understanding, history or context
2. to share information – good, bad or indifferent
3. to seek a solution to a problem, usually at school, that needs to be managed
4. to seek advice, often about managing a home issue
5. to give advice or share expertise.

If the parents and school staff can jointly understand why there is parental engagement, there are a few questions that can build relationships between parents and teachers. Asking the right questions for the right context can build relationships within the school protocols.

Based on my experience I believe there are only three questions, or variations of these questions, that parents should be asking school staff. Similarly, I believe there are only three questions, with variations, that school staff should be asking parents when it comes to communication.

The three questions teachers should ask parents after parents come and meet with the school staff are:

1. **What do you (the parents) need?** This indicates that the teacher wants to listen to the parent, meet their needs and engage them in any resolution.
2. **What do you believe that (the solution to the need) would look like in our class?** This allows the teacher to invite the parent to reflect on their request from the school's viewpoint. The teacher is asking themselves, "Is the parent's request *realistic* and *sustainable*?". The teacher needs both criteria met to commit to the resolution.
3. **Is there anything else I can assist you with?** This gives the parent the opportunity to do a quick mental audit to check if there is anything else they wish to discuss.

The three questions parents should ask teachers after their child has shared a story of something that happened at school are:

1. **What happened at school?** This invites the teacher to explain what happened at school from the teacher's perspective.
2. **What is the school's philosophy or policy on the relevant topic?** This allows the teacher to explain the school's position and practice on the topic.
3. **How can we work together for the benefit of my child/ren?** This indicates that the parents wish to work with the school.

Conversely, when school staff approach parents for a conversation – for example, when they have to give feedback about a child's progress – similar protocols can be put in place. It is reasonable that the staff member makes an appointment for the parent to come and visit a particular time. It is reasonable that the staff member gives the parent some background as to why they're coming in for a conversation. It's reasonable that these communications are done face-to-face. It's also reasonable for the parent to suggest that they only have a certain amount of time to communicate with the staff member. However, if it is a spontaneous conversation, some of these protocols may be loosened to prioritise building a relationship. As stated above, communication is one of the key strategies in building relationships within school communities.

Setting

Another important aspect of communication between parents and staff is the setting in which these conversations take place. When a parent is called to the principal's office it can be quite intimidating. It does add a degree of importance to the conversation when you are asked to meet the principal in their office; however, it may also be appropriate that the conversation takes place in a classroom. Certainly the majority of teacher-parent conversations would take place in a classroom. Schools may have access to a meeting room, and this may be less formal than meeting in the principal's office.

Whatever environment school staff choose to have their conversation with the parents, they should be able to promote relationships without intimidating the parents, remembering that some parents haven't been inside a principal's office since they were at school, and when they were at school they may well have been in the principal's office for not making good choices and will therefore have negative memories. It is quite common when parents are going to meet in the principal's office that they say, "This brings back scary memories of when I was at school". In such cases the principal needs to alleviate any concerns the parent might have about the conversation. Of course, if the matter the parents are being called in to discuss with the school staff is extremely serious, then meeting in the principal's office may be quite appropriate.

Once we have identified a setting for the conversation, it is also important for the school staff to consider the seating arrangements and furniture within that space so that once again they can build a relationship. It might sound pedantic, but the position of desks, chairs and tables in a room can promote relationships or threaten or harm them. Does sitting in front of a huge desk where the principal is seated in a beautiful leather chair and the parent is seated in a small simple chair create a power imbalance? Quite possibly. Does sitting around a coffee table on chairs of all the same size, where it appears we are all in the conversation together, make the conversation more palatable to everybody and hence promote collaboration and trust? Would seating the parents facing a bright window, where they could be distracted by whatever is happening outside, impact how the conversation might unfold? If there are multiple people in a conversation, does a long boardroom promote relationships or does it promote position and power? These are some of the questions school leaders should be asking themselves when they're trying to promote positive relationships within the protocols that they have established for communication. Seating arrangements can promote position and power or help form relationships of collaboration and trust.

How Parents Communicate

When parents and school staff are communicating it is important that both parties understand the appropriate channels for the appropriate topics. For example, if a parent wishes to discuss their child's progress, they should communicate with the child's teacher. Educational progress is a matter for the teacher to address, and hence the parent needs to work directly with the class teacher and not go above them to the deputy principal or principal. If the parent doesn't get satisfaction from the teacher, it is reasonable for them to engage with a member of the leadership team for the same conversation.

If a parent wishes to discuss a school matter which is unrelated to the child's progress, then it is reasonable that the parents discuss it with the relevant staff, be that a deputy or the school principal. The way parents communicate with their child's teacher will enhance that culture of trust and collaboration. If a parent immediately goes to the leadership team for what is a matter for the teacher, that will erode their relationship because it indicates they do not trust their child's teacher – they have gone outside the chain of command. This protocol and expectation needs to be articulated very clearly, usually at the start of the year, by member of the leadership team when briefing parents about plans for the year ahead.

Parent to Parent Communication

Communication between parents within the school body can be one of the most worthwhile and positive experiences parents can have in a school. Conversely, communication between parents can also be some of the most volatile, explosive and damaging experiences within school communities. At this point it is important to remember that parents and teachers are there for the good of the child they have in common. Everything that happens in a school should be for the benefit of the child's education, not for one child but for all children within a particular school setting. While parents only have to worry about the education of their child, school staff have to worry about the education of all students. School teachers may believe they only have to worry about the education of the children for whom they are responsible; that is, the students in their class. However, the leadership team, principal and deputies are responsible for ensuring that all children have access to a high-quality education in their school. Schools need to establish specific protocols for communication between parents so that parents have guidelines within which they can operate to build positive, harmonious relationships. Let's unpack some examples of where communication between parents can be most profitable.

When new families arrive at school, the way they are greeted by school staff and by fellow parents can make or break their first impressions. It's common for schools to have class liaison representatives within the parent body that are charged with making new families welcome at the school. That initial communication can be very welcoming and very encouraging and will set the tone for parent relationships within the school. If a new family gets a phone call and email from the class liaison rep to simply say,

"Welcome to our community. Would you like to get together and have a coffee?", that can be so welcoming for them.

Similarly, when families work together and encourage each other to take on leadership roles within the school, that can be inviting for all parents. Schools rely on parents to volunteer their time and energy. While it may not be possible for individuals to offer all their time and energy, it may be possible for parents to work together to fulfill roles needed within the parent leadership groups – for example, the parents and citizens associations. These are examples of how positive parent relationships and communication can achieve greatness. When schools run large social events such as fetes, trivia nights and big fundraisers, they need parent volunteers to step up and show leadership. The success of such functions rely on parents. If parents can work harmoniously and communicate effectively, then greatness can be achieved both financially and socially for the schools. While the responsibility rests with the school principal or the school board, parent leadership is critical for the success of such activities and events.

However, when parent communication goes awry it can create headaches not only for the parents and the students but also sometimes the staff. There are occasions when parents may feel that liaising directly with fellow parents about what is largely a school matter is appropriate. It is not. For example, if two children are having a dispute during school time, that should be left to the school staff to manage. It is not appropriate for parents to take disciplinary actions for other parents' children into their own hands. It is not appropriate for parents to engage with students who they believe are not treating their child fairly or appropriately.

It is important that the school articulates the necessary protocols for parents to communicate within the school boundaries. What happens outside of school may be beyond the school leadership team's circle of influence. However, if there are matters that are related to school, then communication should happen between school staff and parents or parents and the leadership team. If parents are promoting positive relationships within their own parent community and the communication is constructive and appropriate, that is absolutely fine. However, if they take matters into their own hands regarding managing children's behaviour, that is not appropriate.

Teacher to Student Communication

As children reach the later stages of primary school and move to high school the opportunity for communication between teachers and students increases outside of school time. It is not uncommon for teachers to provide feedback to students via technology about their school work. It is common for high school teachers to provide additional support for groups or individuals of students during lunch breaks or before or after school time. It is critical when these teaching methodologies are put in place that strict protocols are followed so that relationships may be built without any fear of misunderstanding on this communication. For example, the only email addresses that teachers and students should be using are work and school email addresses which are accessible to members of the leadership team and the people who manage school networks.

It is not appropriate for teachers and students to be exchanging mobile phone numbers. There may be rare occasions when that is necessary, but it must be done with the parents' and the school leadership team's full knowledge. It is generally not appropriate, however, and may jeopardise the relationships between parents, staff and students if boundaries are crossed through inappropriate communication. There can be no questions asked about the way adults communicate with students and the messages that adults and students share. It may be deemed acceptable for staff to give feedback to students individually via their school email addresses, but teachers must ensure that they communicate with students in a highly professional manner and do not leave themselves open to any innuendo or question regarding the messages being communicated.

There are no reasons why staff would be sharing any personal information with a student of any nature via email or social media. If a staff member determines that they wish to share a personal story with students collectively or individually, they need to do so in a manner that is highly professional and relevant to the educational journey of the students. For example, sharing what staff members did on the weekend in a social environment is not appropriate.

Staff as Parents

One of the great challenges for staff in school environments is when they are also the parents of students at the school. This is very common in primary schools, where teachers may have their own children at the same school, and hence those teachers are not only staff members, they are also parents. They may have friendly relationships with other parents in the community, and as parents, that is perfectly reasonable. However, they need to be very clear about the boundaries and protocols in which they can operate so that no lines are crossed when communicating between parents, to parents and with parents.

At social events it is common for parents to discuss their children's schooling. Invariably that may include discussing teachers. On such occasions the teacher/parent needs to minimise their input into conversations about their work and especially about their colleagues. The challenge is exacerbated if the teacher/parent hears negative feedback about their colleagues. Do they shut it down? Do they defend their colleague? Do they tell their colleague? Do they tell their principal? These questions emphasise the balancing act that teachers with dual roles face. Teacher/parents need to set their own boundaries to maximise their relationships within practical protocols.

Some teacher/parents make intentional choices to keep their social life separate from their school social networks. Those who do cross that divide need to be astute in articulating their boundaries in communicating with their fellow school parents. This may include setting limits on topics for open discussion and actions they feel comfortable taking when a parent crosses that boundary. It can happen, and teacher/parents need a planned response.

Social engagements are just one of the communication forums available for teacher/parents. Along with the face-to-face communication that happens at social events, there are the numerous social networking sites parents use for public and private communications. Think of the popular social networking sites or communication platforms that parents use and the pitfalls people occasionally encounter. Parents need to respect the professional and personal boundaries that are necessary for teacher/parents to maintain some distance between their work and personal lives. I have often used my work email for direct communication with parents and have also given parents my personal mobile number for use when I am away with work. Never has a parent misused either platform for personal communication.

Email Protocols

Possibly the most common form of professional communication, emailing comes with great possibilities and responsibilities and, sadly, pitfalls. Principals should set reasonable email protocols so communication can be effective in promoting positive relationships. For example, teachers should respond to a parent's email within 48 hours of receiving the message during the working week. This means that a teacher has time to digest the message and formulate an appropriate response. It also means that if a parent sends an email to a parent on the weekend, the parent should expect a response soon after the working week begins. It allows the teacher to have a weekend, without feeling obliged to respond immediately. This does take some training and personal responsibility. Even if the teacher knows the email protocols, it is up to the individual to follow them. Some teachers may choose to respond to emails earlier than expected.

Email protocols are designed to protect teachers from themselves and from unrealistic parental expectations. Teachers who choose to keep some personal time will train themselves to respond within the protocols. School leaders would also be wise to follow these protocols, otherwise emails may rule their lives. With email on smartphones, communication is accessible 24/7. It is not healthy to be continuously responding immediately to emails, so school leaders should be careful, be sensible and set a good example for staff.

One of the great traps when emailing people is the temptation to "reply all". When a group email is distributed it is not uncommon for recipients to hit "reply all" so that their response goes to a wider audience. Frequently this is unnecessary. When responding to an email, parents, teachers and leadership teams need to be prudent in their judgement. When responding to an email they must determine whether the response needs to go to a single recipient or the whole group. I would suggest "reply all" is only necessary during group collaboration or whenever everybody needs to be informed of a decision. By and large, when a group email is distributed the recipients may wish to simply acknowledge the message by responding to the individual sender.

Similarly, when students are distributing emails they need to communicate with the recipients as if they were standing face-to-face and talking to them directly. We do not want students to become keyboard warriors and think it is okay to email their peers in a manner which is disrespectful or contrary to how they would speak to those people face-to-face. Likewise, when students respond to emails they should not hit "reply all" unless it is for the benefit of the whole group. Replying to the sender directly is frequently all that is needed.

When schools receive unsolicited communications from external providers, be it a salesperson or education provider, it is very easy for the recipient not to respond or for the response to be brief and direct. To build relationships it is necessary that any response be polite and respectful while declining the offer, if appropriate. Ignoring emails does not build relationships. Ignoring an email may send a clear message of rejection; however, it is important that unsolicited emails are responded to in a succinct and respectful manner.

Teacher Protocols

Principals are very conscious about building relationships with parents and understand that communication is key. When a principal expects that teachers communicate with parents in a regular and professional way and a teacher struggles to meet these requirements, does this "failure" result in professional guidance and jeopardise staff relationships or is there a degree of latitude allowed?

A child's education is enhanced by a healthy relationship between parents and teachers and it makes good sense to build that relationship. Parents can also be teachers' greatest advocates. Staff who are reluctant to engage with parents in a positive and regular way may require some coaching as to communication methods that are mutually beneficial. Some staff may welcome these coaching sessions as way to improve their professional practice.

While face-to-face communication is preferable, email is often more convenient. Texting and telephone calls are other methods of communication that are often used. These create a more intimate connection but can be risky as they may breach the boundaries necessary to keep the relationship professional. Once a parent and teacher have exchanged phone numbers, it is difficult to prevent their use for personal exchanges despite best intentions.

Scenarios to Consider

Scenario 1

Context: A parent has appeared on the doorstep of the principal's office and demanded to see the principal about the way a teacher has allegedly bullied their child. The parent is refusing to leave the school office until the principal or deputy makes time to see the parent.

Dilemma: How does the school principal manage the situation when they are unaware of the circumstances of the incident but want to build relationships with the parent?

Options: The principal may welcome the parent into their office for a conversation and initially listen to the parent's concerns. The principal or deputy would be wise to make no commitment other than to follow it up with the teacher. The first question the principal asks the parent could be along the lines of, "Have you spoken to your child's teacher about this particular matter?" If they haven't spoken to the child's teacher, the principal may choose to refer the parent to the child's teacher so the teacher and the parent can maintain a relationship before the principal gets more involved.

If for some reason the parent does not feel comfortable addressing the issue with the teacher, the principal or their deputy may offer to mediate a conversation between the teacher and the parent. Of course, the principal and the deputy should be supportive of the teacher. If there are reservations about the teacher's behaviour and the relationship between the parent and the teacher is difficult, it may be necessary to provide guidance to the teacher about how they should conduct themselves in dialogue with the parent. It is not uncommon for school leaders to struggle to support and defend staff members, especially when the staff member has made mistakes. School leaders may not want to appear to choose sides, as the staff member is just seeking the school's leader's support.

The principal of course may refuse to see the parent at the time and insist that the parent make an appointment. This allows the principal some breathing space and the opportunity to seek any background information from relevant staff as to why the parent is in their office. This can work in the principal's favour and can also work against the principal. There are occasions where the parent may calm down and appreciate the breathing space so they can have a conversation with less emotion. There are other occasions where the parent may in fact get more agitated at not having their needs addressed immediately. Only the principal can judge such a scenario and determine how best to address the issue.

Scenario 2

Context: A parent is known to send emotionally charged emails to teachers, particularly if they feel their child has a legitimate concern, in this case alleged unfair treatment. Wanting to defend their response to the student, the teacher chooses to engage in an email debate with the parent. When the debate becomes verbally volatile, both parent and teacher say some things that amount to personal attacks on the other person.

Dilemma: Should the principal publicly agree with the parent and commit to coaching the teacher through the preferred response? Should the principal publicly defend the teacher and present a united voice to the parent's concerns? Or should the principal remain neutral and offer to follow up with the parent after working with the teacher?

Options: When a principal is invited to mediate the conversation between the parent and the teacher, they may feel like they have the professional obligation to support and defend their teacher. This becomes a challenge if the principal disagrees with the teacher's response and may in fact agree with the parent that the teacher was at fault.

The principal can support the teacher by offering to mediate a conversation between the teacher and parent. During this process the principal may be advised to set the rules for the engagement, which may include both parties agreeing to protocols for the conversation. Such protocols may include having an agenda, speaking and listening in turns, recording the agreed outcomes and committing to check in with each other after a set period of time.

The principal can listen to both parties and encourage them to listen to each other with the goal of coming to a position in the best interests of the child. As such, the principal may guide to conversation with probing questions about the needs of each party and the needs of the child.

Scenario 3

Context: Three out of four leadership team members agree with the appointment of a new staff member, yet the dissenting voice feels unheard, despite being present for all deliberations and sharing their opinions in a forthright manner. The dissenting team member feels their opinions are not valued and they walk away, literally leaving the meeting and even the school for a period of time.

Dilemma: The remaining team members need to find a way to move forward. Do they change their opinion to appease the disgruntled team member? Do they confront the individual and attempt to identify the issues and hence a way forward? Or do they ignore the behaviour and hope the individual will rejoin the team when ready, with time and space being an antidote?

Options: When a leadership team aims to work together, it is common for them to meet regularly, probably weekly, to discuss and plan for the school priorities. Each team member has their unique role description, covering school goals such as curriculum, strategic planning, staff management and student behaviour. Sometimes team members may not always agree, and that's okay. In fact diversity of opinions in teams is a strength. However, when a team member takes a difference of opinion as a personal affront or attack, there may be a problem. When that team member chooses to walk away from the situation a resolution needs to be found so the team can function harmoniously.

The team needs to acknowledge that difference of opinions is a strength and that unanimous consensus is not necessary. Ultimately the buck stops with the principal, so if the team can't agree on a common vision then the principal may make the final decision.

Alternately the team may agree that majority decisions are accepted. The team would also need to agree that while diversity of opinion is valued, when the team communicates a message to the staff or parents there will be one common message and the team members will support each other, even if one member may feel at odds with the decision.

If the team is dysfunctional due to one or more team member feeling aggrieved, then more direct conversations seeking a resolution may be necessary. The team can set clear and agreed protocols as a group to meet the professional needs of each team member. There should be clear role descriptions so each team member fulfils their responsibilities without overstepping the mark. If some school leaders have similar titles but distinct responsibilities, role descriptions can eliminate any confusion over individual obligations.

Summary

Both verbal and non-verbal communication are key vehicles when building relationships, and there are numerous modes of communication available to school leaders and parents. Clear messages with common goals for the students should be the priority for relevant parties. Communication also needs to be clear within school staff teams so collaboration is enhanced through cooperation among colleagues. If communication breaks down, the five P's will enhance the opportunity for resolutions. The five P's coupled with the positive relationships should go a long way to building a strong community. Communication is a key element and balancing working within the five P's while promoting harmonious relationships is an important step for creating a high-performing school.

"Rules are made for the guidance of the wise and the strict adherence of fools."

Harry Day, First World War Royal Flying Corps fighter ace

Think of your own COMMUNICATION scenario and do a response analysis

Scenario:

Dilemma:

Options:

Response checklist:
- ☑ **Does the response improve the learning and wellbeing of students, staff and families?**
- ☑ **Workplace health and safety**: Will the action keep people safe?
- ☑ **Transparency**: Do stakeholders understand the rationale for the action?
- ☑ **Best interests of the majority**: Is the action in the best interests of the majority of stakeholders?
- ☑ **Fairness**: Does the action meet the needs of stakeholders?
- ☑ **Practicality and sustainability**: Can the action be done and continue to be done?
- ☑ **Cost-benefit analysis**: Does the cost of the action warrant the outcome?
- ☑ **Legal requirements**: Does the action meet the obligations of relevant legislation?

Chapter 5

CURRICULUM

The main purpose of a school education is for students to be provided with high-quality teaching so they improve their knowledge and skills, particularly in the subjects taught. There are many other benefits to school-based education, including social engagements, independence, confidence, resilience and building friendships. Schools invariably have numerous practices, processes, procedures, protocols and policies associated with curriculum delivery. This chapter unpacks the expectations on teachers in delivering the curriculum and how collaboration is key to successful teaching.

Dead Poets Society, starring Robin Williams, is set in a fictional elite boarding school in the United Kingdom. Williams's character is an English teacher who inspires his students through poetry. Some of his teaching methods are questioned by his colleagues and initially by his students, as his pedagogy is rather unique to motivate his students, while his faculty colleagues are more traditional in their delivery of the curriculum, following the accepted and expected practices.

The students are excited by the way poetry is unpacked to reveal its meaning. The relationship between the teacher and his students is one of trust, collaboration and enquiry. The students trust their teacher, especially when they are invited to engage in learning outside of school boundaries. The students and teacher collaborate in their learning, while asking many questions about content and pedagogy.

Dead Poets Society illustrates how a teacher can teach the curriculum, following the content to be taught, while adding their own unique flavour in delivery. It is a good example of how protocols must be followed in terms of the curriculum that needs to be taught while allowing some creativity from the teacher in how they deliver it. The teacher balanced following the curriculum with teaching the students creatively, which built trusting relationships.

Subjects

The Australian Curriculum Assessment Reporting Authority (ACARA) sets out the expected subjects to be taught in Australian schools. There are three dimensions to the Australian Curriculum: learning areas, general capabilities and cross-curriculum priorities. These all contribute to a well-rounded education of all Australian students, providing the knowledge, understanding and skills needed for life and work in the 21st century.

ACARA has developed the Foundation – Year 10 Australian Curriculum in the following learning areas: English, Mathematics, Science, Humanities and Social Sciences, The Arts, Technologies and Health and Physical Education. In faith-based schools Religion may be taught as the ninth subject. There are numerous languages that may be taught in schools across Australia to supplement the teaching of English, including Arabic, Auslan (sign language for people with hearing impairment), Chinese, Framework for Aboriginal Languages and Torres Strait Languages, Framework for Classical Languages, French, German, Hindi, Indonesian, Italian, Japanese, Korean, Modern Greek, Spanish, Turkish and Vietnamese.

Each school has a degree of autonomy as to how the curriculum is delivered. Schools also have a degree of autonomy regarding school hours as long as the subjects are taught according to the minimum number of hours that are allocated to each subject. The allocation of hours for each subject are described in the table, provided by the Queensland Curriculum Assessment Authority in 2021.

Hours per week over 37–40 weeks per year						35–38 weeks/ yr
Learning area	P–3	3–4	5–6	7–8	9	10
English		250–270	203–220	185–200	111–120	111–120	105–114
Mathematics		166–180	166–180	148–160	111–120	111–120	105–114
Science		37–40	64–70	64–70	92–100	111–120	105–114
Health & PE		74–80	74–80	74–80	74–80	74–80	70–76
Humanities and Social Sciences	History	18–20	37–40	37–40	46–50	46–50	43–48
	Geography	18–20	37–40	37–40	46–50	46–50	43–48
	Economics and business			18–20	18–20	46–50	43–48
	Civics and citizenship		18–20	18–20	18–20	18–20	17–19
The Arts		37–40	46–50	46–50	74–80	74–80	70–76
Languages			46-50		74-80	74-80	70-76
Technologies	Design and technology	18–20	37–40	55–60	74–80	37–40	35–38
	ICT					37–40	35–38

As the core business of any teacher is to provide high-quality teaching for all students, it is imperative that teachers follow the school expectations, practices, protocols, procedures, processes and policies to teach the Australian Curriculum. This means that teachers are expected to thoroughly plan and document what they will be teaching and how they will be teaching so the school has an accurate record of the content being covered as required. Planning for all subjects should be documented, including the adjustments made for students who require differentiation. The planning should be saved in a central repository, such as a school portal, that is accessible by at least the teaching and leadership staff. Many schools also share their planning overview with parents so the parents can support the school in supporting the students' learning.

Many schools are moving towards short cycles of planning with units of work that are only three to four weeks long. This allows teachers to be instructional leaders and to be very specific about the content, strategies and pedagogy they are using to see improvements in students learning. Short cycles of planning are recommended as they allow the teacher to see the impact of their teaching very quickly. If there is minimal improvement in students' work, teachers can adjust their teaching to accommodate the learning progress of the students (Sharratt and Fullan, 2012).

Planning

When teachers are planning their teaching strategies and lesson sequence, they are well served to plan to explain to the students what an expected level of work looks like and, ideally, what above-expected and well-above-expected work looks like. This approach allows students to plan to achieve the highest level they are capable of. Modern practices would suggest that teachers are well served in their planning process, and their teaching process, to use learning intentions – that is, what they hope the students will learn from each lesson or each unit of work – and success criteria, which are the outcomes they anticipate the students will display if they have grasped a concept and can perform a task. These are modern practices implemented in many schools that allow the planning, teaching and assessment process to be very transparent. Transparency is one of the great allies for all teachers when trying to balance the five P's and building harmonious, productive relationships. When teachers use learning intentions and success criteria they are being transparent –they are following the five P's while building relationships with their students, colleagues and the parents of their students.

Planning is typically done in teaching teams, with teachers of the same year level working as a collaborative team, often under the supervision of a curriculum leader. Curriculum leaders may be called head of curriculum, primary learning leader or deputy principal curriculum depending on the context. These leaders ensure the curriculum is being covered and that teachers are documenting and recording the curriculum they plan to teach. Ideally resources, strategies, content, potentially the sequencing of lessons and assessments will be discussed during these planning sessions. Planning sessions also give teachers the opportunity to share their expertise and to tweak units that have been taught previously but remain relevant. Teachers may also take the opportunity to explore ways they can enhance the learning experience through excursions or incursions. It also allows the teachers to use the Australian Curriculum documents to ensure that they are covering the achievement standards as set out by the Australian government.

Teaching

Following planning, teachers then go about teaching what they have planned, which requires them to think about the lesson sequence and any resources they may need. It will have them concentrating on the individual students as well as the whole group. They'll have to plan activities that are engaging to enhance the experience. They will have to plan how they would differentiate for the diverse range of learners in their class. They may need to factor in the use of support staff, such as a learning support/inclusion teacher and teacher aides, to accommodate individual learning needs. The implementation of the teachers' planning is their core business. It is when they work with the students to ensure they learn and understand content, capabilities, processes and skills. This is the time when teachers need to be aware of the amount of time that lessons will take so that the allocated hours for each subject are in fact covered.

It is also the time when teachers may choose to teach individual subjects or to integrate subjects. As long as the achievement standards in the Australian Curriculum are taught and students have the opportunity to display their ability, then teachers are doing their job. Current pedagogy would suggest that students may work in groups after a period of instruction from the teachers. There may be the need for teachers to accommodate the use of technology in their lessons. In primary schools many students now use one-to-one devices to enhance the learning experience. There is certainly a place for paper and pencil work as well, but the device or the pencil is only as good as the person using it.

The teacher may also need to consider any hands-on resources they will use, especially for subjects such as maths and science, where using manipulatives certainly enhances children's learning experience. Young children certainly learn by doing and engaging as opposed to just paper and pencil or computer work. It is important therefore that teachers use experiences to enhance learning. Literature is also a vital resource when it comes to providing high-quality learning opportunities. Rich texts can enhance the literacy of any subject, and students can broaden their use of language and literacy across all subjects.

Assessment

The teaching cycle includes the assessment journey, and there are two types of assessments that teachers should be following: formative and summative assessment. In formative assessment teachers keep samples of work throughout a unit of work, which means the assessment process is ongoing as the students continue to learn and develop. Summative assessment is work that tends to be done at the end of a period of teaching. It is very common in high schools, where they have exam blocks, while not as common in primary schools anymore. Certainly both forms of assessment are relevant in the educational journey of students. Assessment must reflect the work that teachers have taught. Hence when teachers are planning, they do need to think about the achievement standards they are covering and how they will assess that work. Teachers must give students the opportunity to demonstrate their progress and their achievements. Assessments need to be a key part of planning units of work.

There are various assessment tools that are standardised, which some schools choose to use, and there are some mandated assessment tools, which all schools are expected to use. The National Assessment Program Literacy and Numeracy, known as NAPLAN, is in virtually all schools across Australia. It is a point-in-time test for students in grades 3, 5, 7 and 9, whereby they are assessed in numeracy, reading and writing. The results are made public and often scrutinised by education systems, school leaders and the community, especially parents when comparing schools for their children. There are other assessment tools that schools often adopt, such as the ACER tests, which are commonly referred to as PAT-M, the Progressive Assessment Tests for Maths, and PAT-R, the Progress Assessment Test for Reading.

Another monitoring tool often used in schools and school systems is the PM benchmark for reading. PM benchmarking is often preceded by letter/sound knowledge and concepts about print, which then lead into children being assessed in reading using the PM levels. Some education systems collect this data on a regular basis so they can ensure their schools are continuing to improve through explicit improvement agendas. While some teachers find it difficult to give young children assessment tasks, it is vital that we track the literacy progress of students from a very early age. Research indicates that students who are not capable readers by the end of year 3 may struggle academically throughout their schooling. These foundation skills are the most reliable predictor of longer-term educational outcomes and personal and economic wellbeing (House of Representatives Education and Training Committee 2002). The emphasis on literacy in the early years, prep and grades 1, 2 and 3 is key to students' success in the following years.

While school leaders are mandated by their education authorities to participate in NAPLAN and must follow the strict protocols directed by the commonwealth government, they have a degree of autonomy as to how

NAPLAN is promoted, prepared for and prioritised within their schools. This is a balancing act of emphasising its importance and following the protocols while managing the human response from teachers, parents and students.

We live in a literate world where language is present in many forms in our day-to-day life. Be it the spoken word, the printed word or illustrations which convey message and meaning, we live in a world where language is central to our methods of communication. Hence children must have a sound knowledge of language from a very early age. Teachers must plan, teach, assess, monitor and track students' literacy progress from a very early age.

Many schools have introduced what are commonly known as data walls. These walls often display the work of students from across the whole school. Such data walls may reflect the English literacy progress and possibly the maths progress of each student. Data walls allow the leadership team and teachers to be able to see progress, not just of the whole class but of individual students as well. They also emphasise that students' progress is not solely the class teacher's responsibility. As we work in schools, which are communities, the progress of all students is the responsibility of all teachers! Collaboration, collegial support and professional dialogue are critical if teachers are to see student progress. While data walls may be seen as threatening by some teachers – some may even say they are embarrassing for people – students are very attuned as to their abilities and their classmates' abilities. And while data walls are not for public consumption, they are certainly available for teachers to study and to use as a way to follow their students' progress. Some teachers have data walls inside their classroom, which allows students to observe their own progress and even set their own goals for levels they aim to reach.

Data walls are often available on an electronic database as well. Schools might have a repository of all students' progress which is available to staff.

Academic data tells a story, and teachers need to be data informed – not necessarily data driven but certainly data informed – as to our practice so that we can track progress, monitor practice and see improvement. Certainly the literacy and numeracy progress of students will be tracked and monitored through tools such as NAPLAN. And while some educators struggle to see the value of NAPLAN, it does serve a purpose, even though the tool itself may be questioned. It is one measure that is publicly available for all schools, and for better or worse, families and school systems do compare results across schools and education authorities.

Reporting

Following the assessment process is the opportunity to report to students and parents, and throughout the year school systems are also required to report assessment results to the education authorities. Teachers need to keep accurate records of student progress so that they can fulfill their assessment requirements. The most important feedback of course is to the students so they can continue to learn and improve. Providing feedback to parents about their children's progress is also vitally important. While this formally happens only a couple of times a year in most schools, parents may ask for feedback on their child's progress as frequently as they choose. Teachers are well served by providing parents regular feedback about their children's progress.

Many schools have a philosophy of "no surprises" for parents and leadership teams when it comes to reporting. That means that teachers need to be very thorough in their provision of regular feedback to students and parents so that when the formal report cards are prepared there are no surprises for anybody. In their assessment requirements Australian government schools are mandated to use a five-point scale. Frequently this is where the value "C" is what children are expected to be able to do during that year level, "B" indicates above expected and "A" indicates well above expected, whereas "D" indicates below expected and "E" indicates well below expected.

Schools generally have explicit instructions as to how parent-teacher interviews will be conducted. In high schools it's not uncommon for schools to ask families to book online and have very brief meetings with individual teachers for their child's progress summary reports – this is like speed dating for school parent-teacher interviews. In primary schools it's more common that teachers will allow greater time for each interview as they will be discussing the majority of the subjects. These interviews are usually accompanied by samples of the student's work, and in some cases students may lead the interviews so that they are able to share their progress with their teachers and their parents. It is the student's learning journey, so it makes a lot of sense for the students to be a key player in the reporting process. This is even more relevant if goals are set for the student during these conversations, as the student should be a part of the dialogue when setting objectives for their learning improvement. This approach is quite foreign to many teachers; however, it is becoming more common in schools.

Reporting is providing a formal document as a record of feedback for students about their progress. Feedback is a gift which educators and students alike should welcome. Feedback helps educators and students improve. Now, while schools may mandate the reporting process, what and how the message is delivered is up to the individual teacher. Report cards may be consistent in their format within a school and instructions may be explicitly delivered to teachers as to how report should be completed, but the wording of report cards will be left to the individual teacher. The delivery of the spoken message to the parents will also be left to the teacher's discretion. How a teacher will deliver an honest appraisal of a student's report will vary greatly. How a teacher will deliver good news to a family regarding their child's progress may also vary from a teacher who has to deliver news that may disappoint the family who may have hoped for greater progress. Teachers have an obligation to be honest.

In delivering the message of a student's progress teachers need to be able to justify and rationalise their decisions, hence samples of work are critical when explaining a student's progress. The final result is only one piece of the puzzle that teachers need to explain. It's important that a teacher can say to parents that the child started at point "X" and has now reached point "Y" with samples of work indicating their progress. This is where data is critical to justify results. And while parents are discouraged from comparing their child's results to another student's results, it does happen. Teachers need to encourage parents to shift their thinking from focusing on the final result to focusing on the progress. A child may still be performing below their peers and yet may have made tremendous progress – they are learning! A child may still be performing exceedingly well by virtue of natural gifts yet may not have made a lot of progress. Teachers and parents must focus on progress for student's achievements. This can be said about academic performance and sporting performance as well as creative performance. Teachers must encourage students to continue to improve, to continue to do their best and to set themselves goals for achievement which may motivate them to continue to improve.

Teacher Autonomy

The sections above outline the five P's teachers are expected to follow. So where is the latitude for teachers to be creative and add their own unique style to the teaching and learning process? This question is often asked by teachers who feel that the five P's are too restrictive. There is a tension and a balancing act required by school leaders to allow teachers to be creative individuals and to enhance the learning process through their own unique style while following school procedures, practices, processes, protocols and policies. Research by Hargreaves and O'Connor (2018) has indicated that procedures are necessary to build relationships. Hence, teachers need to be able to follow those five P's to build relationships with their students and to build relationships with the parents.

If teachers follow the processes that allow for high-quality teaching and learning, then parents and students will have confidence in the teachers and teachers will have confidence in the relationships that allow them to do their job to the best of their ability. When teachers maintain the required practices and procedures necessary to provide high-quality teaching and learning they promote harmonious positive relationships within schools.

It is important that teachers can show their own individuality when teaching. Every teacher has their own unique style in the way they deliver content and process. Teachers will have their own unique skill sets and their own strengths when teaching the curriculum. In high schools teachers usually teach subjects they are passionate about and skilled in. Primary school teachers are generalists; that is, they teach the majority of subjects themselves. Specialist teachers might be employed for some subjects, such as health and physical education, music, the arts and languages, but the majority of the subjects are left to the primary school teacher to teach. Within those general subjects individual teachers will have individual strengths. Some teachers may prefer to teach English as opposed to maths. Others may have a passion for teaching science. Wherever our teachers' passions lie, they will have their own style in delivering the curriculum for the students and with the students, so there does need to be a degree of latitude given to the delivery of the curriculum so that teachers can shine. Teachers who are passionate about a subject will probably teach it brilliantly. Teachers who are mandated to teach in a particular way may struggle to bring the degree of enthusiasm necessary to motivate students.

Andrea Levinson, Chief Operating Officer of Executive Performance Partners, explains that leaders should be able to operate with freedom within boundaries. This creates some autonomy and flexibility for people to operate within the five P's. It allows people to have individual variety in their delivery, while not deviating from the common core business, in this case providing high-quality teaching and learning for high-performing schools, which is precisely the balancing act that is the basis of this book. Teachers and school leaders need to work within the five P's as mandated by their employing authorities, while using their own unique skills to develop the school mission of high-quality teaching and learning. Some teachers are more maverick in their implementation of the mandated practices while maintaining a high standard of outcomes from the students.

When asked how to prioritise tasks, the Head of Department at a Yeronga State High School in Brisbane, Domini Roblin, said she responds to what is urgent (time sensitive) and what affects the wellbeing of the students. If students' wellbeing is jeopardised, learning becomes difficult. Teachers and school leaders must ensure students' wellbeing so learning can be prioritised.

Support Staff

Another part of the teaching and learning processes is the work that support staff can provide so that all students can access the curriculum. Schools have various additional personnel who they employ to support all students' access to the curriculum. Specialised teachers in learning support or inclusion are employed as their expertise can add advanced skills in supporting students to do the best they can in learning. These teachers work in a variety of models. The withdrawal model is the tried and tested model where students are withdrawn from their mainstream classroom and put into small groups with intensive intervention provided by a learning support teacher or an intervention teacher. In another model these teachers may work in class alongside the class teacher and provide specialised strategies and intervention which meet the needs of these students while learning with their class.

School officers or teacher aides are employed to work with students in class, which allows the class teacher more time to work with other students. It is not uncommon for school officers to work with students with the greatest needs, though this is not ideal. School officers or teacher aides should be employed to work with students who are capable, independent learners who may need some supervision or some consolidation of work. Teachers are the most skilled and qualified instructional leaders in a class, and hence they should work with the students with the greatest needs. This does prompt the big question of how school leaders give explicit instructions that teachers should work with the students who have the greatest need while school officers and teacher aides work with other students.

Scenarios to Consider

Scenario 1

Context: A school officer is expected to work with a student with significant learning needs. They are asked to prepare resources or activities to support the student's learning in an individual subject the student is struggling with. The school officer feels out of their depth and is reluctant to express their limitations to the teacher for fear of not being seen as confident or competent to do their job.

Dilemma: How does the school officer follow the teacher's instruction, knowing it is against the school leader's instructions and not in the best interests of the student? Should the school officer approach the teacher to express their reservations about having to work with the student with significant learning needs? Should they approach a deputy or another member of the school leadership team and express their concerns, understanding that it may jeopardise the relationship with the class teacher? Should the school officer seek professional development so they feel more skilled in addressing the needs of these students? Or should the school officer express their desire to work with other students who are more aligned to their skills?

Options: The school officer should seek clarity around their role from the class teacher. They would also be well served to seek clarity from the leadership team as to their expectations of all school officers within the school in terms of which students they should work with. Having sought clarity from school leaders, the school officer may then seek support from the school leaders to clarify the role to all teaching staff and all school officers to ensure consistency of practice within the school.

We do need the most skilled and qualified and trained personnel working with the students with the greatest needs and that is the class teacher. School officers serve a valuable role in working with individuals and small groups, but they need to have the training and the upskilling to work with needy students. School leaders need to balance the skill sets of their teachers and the skill sets of their school offices to ensure all children can access the curriculum and high-quality teaching and learning.

Scenario 2

Context: A principal is charged with ensuring their school follows the mandated assessment requirements, which use a five-point scale. A very experienced teacher finds it difficult to publicly give students results well below or well above the expected level when reporting on student achievement. When the principal asks the teacher if they use a five-point scale or are more comfortable using a three-point scale, they say that a three-point scale is what they generally use.

Dilemma: Becoming aware that teachers are more comfortable using a three-point scale means the principal is in fact needing to remind the staff of the obligations set out in the Australian Curriculum. Having said that, the principal also wants to encourage collegial support and high-quality teaching practices within a harmonious, productive environment. The principal has to follow the expected assessment practices while encouraging professional growth in their teachers and within their teaching teams. How do they manage this balancing act?

Options: Ideally principals, deputies and heads of curriculum (HOCs) meet with teachers on a regular basis to discuss their planning and their students' achievements. It is during these conversations that staff can discuss the progress from the monitoring tools – for example, PM Benchmarks (reading levels), PAT-R (reading) and PAT-M (maths) tests – that reflect the students' work and the teacher's practices. During these conversations school leaders may identify a particular teacher who is only using a three-point scale through the breadth of results their class is displaying.

If the teacher acknowledges the limitations of their assessment, then the school leaders need to ask some pertinent questions. For example, is the teacher providing enough scope in the work and the assessment tasks for students to display above-expected and well-above-expected results, which are necessary for a five-point scale? Is the teacher comfortable making professional judgements about the students' ability which may reflect well above or well below if students have not grasped the concept and are not performing at the expected level?

The principal needs to work through the importance of the five-point scale and the educational expectations that a five-point assessment scale must be used. Follow-up conversations may be necessary. School leaders can reflect back on students' previous work samples, from previous units of work, or previous weeks and months, to determine if, they are in fact capable of performing at well above or above the standard. Monitoring the teacher's assessment tasks will be important, which the head of curriculum will probably do as part of their role.

Scenario 3

Context: A school leader has a personal philosophy about the model of education that they believe is best suited for the community. They believe that multi-age classes are best suited to modern teaching practices. The school leader has several staff who feel confident and competent to teach within this model, while other teachers feel less confident and competent. Additionally, some families have decided to leave the school as they disagree with the principal's vision for the teaching model.

Dilemma: The principal must decide between moving forward following their individual philosophy or following the popular beliefs of the school community, which may be less informed than the principal. How can the school leader direct the teachers and parents towards the best model of teaching for the school when there are a variety of skills and confidence levels among the teaching staff?

Options: As school leaders are charged with acting in the best interests of all students and staff, choosing a model of teaching for all is a dangerous practice. It is not possible to ensure that one model suits everyone's teaching and learning styles.

Firstly, school leaders should be willing to listen and learn, as all educators should. They are also expected to lead. If they want their staff to learn and follow their lead, then how they make a decision regarding models of teaching is important. Seeking staff input as to their competency and confidence will be a place to start. If there is the capacity for multiple models of teaching within the same school that meet the preference of the school leaders, teachers and families, that is a win-win.

Scenario 4

Context: A teacher is planning an end-of-year excursion, which on paper appears to be a day filled with fun for the students and staff. The teacher seeks the approval of the leadership team, with the rationale that the students have researched the costs associated with the excursion.

Dilemma: The school leader has to decide to approve the excursion or disappoint the students and staff. Does the leadership team approve the excursion when they believe the excursion is simply a fun day to celebrate the end of the year? Does the leadership team approve a trip without curriculum links and hence instruct the finance secretary to not claim back the GST associated with school excursions?

Options: A member of the school leadership team needs to follow this up with the relevant teachers after the team has reached an agreed position on the issue. The teachers would be asked to explain their rationale for the excursion, as described on the risk assessment, so the school leaders can appreciate the position of the teachers. The school leader then has to decide if the excursion has legitimate curriculum links and hence the school can claim the GST back, saving the parents some money. Alternately, the school doesn't claim the GST, pays the full amount and charges the parents accordingly.

Summary

All schools in Australia are expected to follow the curriculum as prescribed by the Australian government. It mandates hours per subject, compulsory subjects across the year levels while allowing great flexibility for leaders and employing authority as to how the curriculum will be delivered. There is mandatory assessment (NAPLAN) in all schools, which allows for some standardised testing and comparative data across schools. And within every school, teachers have a degree of autonomy to deliver the curriculum with as much skill and passion as possible.

School leaders have a degree of autonomy when determining school teaching models, school timetables, some of the subjects that may be taught and how best to resource the school to provide high-quality teaching and learning. This authority that school leaders may discharge comes with the need to balance building trusting, positive relationships with all key stakeholders while driving curriculum improvements for all staff and students.

"Verba volant, scripta manent." (Words fly away, writings remain.)

Latin saying, *The Hater*

Think of your own CURRICULUM scenario and do a response analysis

Scenario:

Dilemma:

Options:

Response checklist:
- ☑ **Does the response improve the learning and wellbeing of students, staff and families?**
- ☑ **Workplace health and safety**: Will the action keep people safe?
- ☑ **Transparency**: Do stakeholders understand the rationale for the action?
- ☑ **Best interests of the majority**: Is the action in the best interests of the majority of stakeholders?
- ☑ **Fairness**: Does the action meet the needs of stakeholders?
- ☑ **Practicality and sustainability**: Can the action be done and continue to be done?
- ☑ **Cost-benefit analysis**: Does the cost of the action warrant the outcome?
- ☑ **Legal requirements**: Does the action meet the obligations of relevant legislation?

Chapter 6

School Rules and Parent Relationships

The American Federation of Teachers suggests that the relationship between a child's parents and their teacher is a key factor for their success at school. As such creating a culture of trust, collaboration and enquiry between the parents and the teachers is key to ensuring a child will achieve their best at school (American Federation of Teachers 2007). Parents seem more involved in their children's education these days post COVID-19. They have had experience in supporting their children's learning at home and many have maintained an active role in their children's learning. Parents are more informed about education in our current climate than they were even 10 years ago.

While teachers generally welcome parental involvement in children's education, teachers also value being respected and parents who understand the boundaries between teacher responsibility and parental responsibilities. This chapter unpacks the processes, practices, protocols, procedures and policies that are necessary to create a culture of trust, collaboration enquiry to create high-performing schools and build positive relationships. Parents can't achieve a high-quality education for their children without teachers, and teachers can't provide a high-quality education for children without their parents. They need to work together.

The *Green Book* is inspired by the story of African American classical and jazz pianist Don Shirley. While on tour in the 1960s, Shirley is driven around by Italian American Frank "Tony Lip" Vallelonga, who also acts as his bodyguard. Various interactions between Shirley and his hosts typify discrimination in the deep south of America at the time. The story highlights the great divide in some parts of the country and the difference an individual made in breaking down some barriers by standing up for what is morally right.

In the south, Shirley is found in a gay encounter with a white man at a pool, and Tony bribes the officers to prevent the musician's arrest. Later, the two are arrested after a police officer pulls them over late at night in a sundown town. Tony punches the officer after being insulted. While they are incarcerated, Shirley asks to call his lawyer and uses the opportunity to reach Attorney General Robert F. Kennedy, who pressures the governor, and subsequently the station officers to release them.

On the night of the final performance on tour in Birmingham, Alabama, Don is refused entry into the whites-only dining room of the country club where he has been hired to perform. Tony threatens the owner, and Shirley refuses to play since they refuse to serve him in the room with his audience. Tony and Shirley leave the venue and instead have dinner at a predominantly black blues club, where Shirley joins the band on the piano. Tony and Shirley head back north to try to make it home by Christmas Eve. Tony invites Shirley to have dinner with his family, but he declines and returns to his own home. Sitting alone in his home, Shirley decides to go back to Tony's home, where he is surprisingly but warmly greeted by Tony's extended family.

This movie shows the prejudice that existed in society and still exists today in countries around the world. It describes how protocols that dictate human behaviour in some societies can be harmful to people, and emphasises the need to build relationships within protocols. The era in which this movie is set had many rules which dictated what were acceptable human interactions. The rules of the time were challenged by the bodyguard, which ultimately led to understanding, tolerance and acceptance of difference. Rules should be there to keep people safe, not inhibit relationships.

Relationships within a school setting are key ingredients to ensure educational provisions are valued by the community. How students relate to each other; how parents relate to each other; how staff relate to each other and relate to parents; and how leaders relate to students, staff and families are all examples of important relationships within the school environment.

Invariably within a school environment there are going to be a variety of family models, different values expressed by parents and staff, different expectations placed on students by teachers and diversity in the home lives of the students. These variables add to the rich tapestry of society, of which schools are a microcosm. With such diversity, how is it possible to have processes, protocols, procedures, policies and practices that cater for the needs of everyone while building positive relationships? It must be a balancing act.

What about some of the basic school rules that principals employ to create the high standard of education they wish to promote within their school? Some of these rules result in conformity. Some of these rules are based on workplace health and safety so that the welfare of staff and students can be maintained. Some rules are based on communication protocols. Parents and staff may work together for the welfare and education of the children, but does one size fit all?

Schools have many protocols, policies, procedures, practices and processes which may cause confusion. Conversely, they may also provide explicit rules to follow. Do schools rely on the common-sense approach of staff and families? On occasions, yes. Following are some examples of topics that often require clear distinct protocols to ensure the education of students is be enhanced and their welfare remains the highest priority while on a school site.

Safe Arrival and Departure at School

One of the great challenges in managing a school site is to coordinate the safe arrival and departure of all students, staff and families. This usually results in protocols being developed to ensure that arrival and pick up routines of all students is clearly communicated to the parents and that parents follow those protocols. When the procedures are known and followed, everyone can arrive and depart safely. If there is a deviation from the accepted practices, chaos and confusion may result and the safety of people can be threatened. When parents and carers fail to follow the carpark procedures, is there scope to bend the guidelines to maintain and build relationships, or do the protocols outweigh the human connections?

In the current climate, where schools are having to navigate changes in protocols as a result of parents not being allowed on site due to the pandemic, it is not uncommon that confusion reigns when parents are asked to change their routines. Even without the pandemic and without changes to protocols, parents are asked to follow the protocols for the safety and wellbeing of all members of the school community. It is not just members of the school community who are being looked after, members of the public also need to be sure that their local community is a safe environment as they access their own private properties that are close to schools.

In the COVID-19 world in which we have lived and educated students, with parents delivering and collecting students, we have had to follow the advice of government health advisors and the school. Waiting outside the school grounds, wearing masks, practising physical distancing, signing in via QR codes or other ways are examples of behaviours expected of carers in and around schools.

On occasions parents may intentionally flaunt the rules and show complete disregard for them. As a principal or deputy, what could and should you do to keep everyone safe? In all reality there is a limit to the school leader's influence, especially if the carers are breaching protocols outside the school boundaries. For example, when carers are waiting outside school grounds and are not wearing a mask nor physically distancing themselves from other carers, can the school leaders enforce the rules? I very much doubt it.

On school grounds there is far greater capacity to enforce the rules. School leaders can ask, request and explain the rationale for the rules. If after all that the carer still refuses to wear the mask, what can the principal do? To the letter of the law the principal could issue a breach notice and exclude the parent from school grounds for an extended period. Would they seriously do so, and would it make a difference? To enforce any rule, there has to be the capacity to enforce sanctions for breaching the rule.

Nowadays it appears that there are fewer ways that rules can be enforced for minor breaches. So how do principals and school leaders manage the situations when families openly flaunt and break protocols of safe arrival and departure? Do principals speak directly to the people who are breaking the rules? Or do they put countless reminders in newsletters and hope that the people who are breaking the rules will in fact read it and adhere to the message? Should principals name and shame families, list numberplates in the newsletter and publicly identify families who are breaking the rules? These are some of the choices principals face when families show disregard for the wellbeing and welfare of other families and students or are just looking after their own families.

The bottom line is that families and staff need to work together in a culture of trust and collaboration for the welfare of everybody. If there are issues where protocols and procedures are challenged, broken or disregarded, questions need to be asked, not accusations made. Through questioning we can identify a context and a rationale for a behaviour, which can then be rectified.

Medication and First Aid at School

The distribution of medication at school must follow very strict protocols so that students can have access to their medication when required and to ensure that the students do not have access to medication that is not theirs. Those protocols must be adhered to and must be followed with very few exceptions. There are always exceptions, however, and these exceptions can help build relationships. They are rare, but they do exist. The distribution of medication for children with severe or serious illnesses may in fact be lifesaving. Children with a variety of medical conditions are part of our schools, and these children must be cared for very carefully so that a safe environment for them can be guaranteed.

When children receive injuries at school there must be clear and distinct protocols for communicating this to families. If a child receives a head injury at school, for example, there must be protocols by which staff can communicate this to their family so that it can be monitored and followed up if required. Does this mean every head injury gets a phone call to home? In some schools, yes. Does it mean that every head injury gets a phone call to an ambulance, and who determines who rings the ambulance? Does it mean that a head injury will be reported to a designated and trained first aid officer for them to make a decision? Where does the buck stop, who is responsible for making those decisions and how do we ensure consistency of practice? Once again we are establishing protocols, procedures, policies, practices and processes to ensure a high level of education in a safe environment for all students.

Uniformity

There are many rules in schools that are designed to promote conformity and pride in the school. Haircuts are one such expectation that schools often have regulations about. This can cause challenges if it is gender based or if it is gender neutral. Do the same rules apply to boys and girls? And does the length of a haircut represent the values and philosophy of the school leaders, the philosophies of the majority of staff or the values and philosophies of the school governing board?

Wearing the correct school uniform is an expectation in most schools. But who sets the uniform, and who sets the consequence for failure to wear the uniform? In a primary school setting are we punishing primary school age children when it is in fact the parents who have allowed the children to come to school in the incorrect uniform? We can't punish the parents for disregarding the school rules. Similarly, with haircuts, should we punish a child for having an inappropriate haircut, which is a value judgement of the leadership team, when in fact the parents allow the child to get the haircut?

The Netflix series *Elite* sees a teenage female student wearing a hijab in honour of her religion. On her first day the principal threatened her with expulsion if she wore the hijab the following day. The student said that it should be respected and asked why it wasn't considered an accessory in the same way wearing a watch would be seen as an accessory. The student removed the hijab so she could attend the school. This raises the important issue of whether or not cultural symbols are recognised and accepted by society, and in particular by schools. If such symbols breach school protocols, how should and could school leaders respond? Cultural and religious symbols are two examples of diversity that are visible in society and schools and may challenge the five P's of the school.

There are also occasions where children with diverse learning needs may challenge the uniform policy or in fact may require an exception to the uniform code. To identify students with diverse needs in the playground, it is common practice for the students to wear an identifying feature on their uniform, such as a band around their hat. Students with a medical condition may need to wear a bracelet to easily identify them. Staff and parents generally accept and embrace such measures to keep the students safe, even though they might technically breach a uniform policy. There are occasions when transparency is necessary yet not as easy to explain when students appear to be breaking the policy without an obvious reason.

Consistency of Practice

The setting and following of rules not only relies on parent-teacher communication, it also relies on a consistent philosophy and rationale for these behaviours and protocols. Rules are designed to promote the culture of the school, which then creates a positive environment for high-quality teaching and learning – the educational output of the school. Interestingly enough, the behaviours that parents will tolerate and accept from their children in small primary schools they will not tolerate from their children in private high schools. It is not uncommon for students to stretch the boundaries in wearing a uniform or fashionable hairstyles at primary school, yet when they move to high school they will not question the rules. I ask the question: why do parents believe it is okay to flaunt the rules in a primary school but not okay to challenge those rules in a high school? It might be a case of why parents test those rules in a government school but will not flaunt them in a private school? For example, parents may not value punctuality in primary schools or government schools yet will be very diligent in having their children be at school on time in private schools. It may be because the sanctions of the private schools have greater impact. Similarly, some parents may question the strict uniform policy or homework practices in primary schools while being very accepting when their children get to private high schools.

Again, how do we build relationships when we are setting high standards for students while trying to maintain relationships with the parent body and respect the individual rights of families to represent their own value systems? This is the balancing act principals face every day.

Separated Families

When separated couples have a child at school there are numerous topics they need to navigate with the school to ensure their obligations, both to the school and to their children, are met. When staff host parent-teacher meetings the management of separated couples may present some issues. There are at least two types of parent-teacher evenings: the general evening where the teacher meets the parents all together and shares the plans for the year and the individual parent-teacher meetings to discuss a child's progress. Should schools have protocols to manage these engagements?

At the general parent-teacher meetings, usually at the start of the year, separated parents should ideally manage their attendance so they can both hear the message from the teacher and/or principal. Whether the separated parents sit together or apart should be up to them. Parents must remain professional in their conduct at school meetings. If topics are discussed that need further exploration and negotiation between the couple, then they may need time to work through these issues, many of which we will discuss here.

For example, when teachers or school leaders need to communicate with the parents, is the school expected to send identical messages to both parents? Court orders may dictate communication expectations in so far as both parties will receive the same correspondence at approximately the same time. So then who makes the decisions when parental permission is required for school functions such as a class excursion or a school camp? Again, the court orders may specify how and who makes such decisions – but not always, and herein lies a possible dilemma.

Similar dilemmas include deciding how a school responds when the parent with custody of the child is unavailable to collect the child if the child is unwell and needs medical attention. The court orders may not have specified what happens on such occasions, in which case the school staff have to determine the best course of action based on what is in the child's best interests. School staff may be using the criteria of the welfare of the child as the basis for breaching protocols. While it seems improbable that parents would use their children to make a point with their previous partners, it does happen, which leaves the school being the main carer on occasions.

Another issue separated parents need to negotiate with the school is the financial responsibility that comes with education. Both government and non-government schools have expenses. Non-government schools often have far greater financial requirements from parents, especially including school fees. The instructions included in court orders provided to separated families regarding financial responsibilities to the school may vary. Court orders need to be explicit and may list the individual school expenses so that each parent understands their commitments. For example, school expenses may include fees, levies, uniforms, books, excursions, camps, computers, music, sport and potentially numerous extra curricula opportunities. Some of these are optional experiences available to students, while others are compulsory. Legal advice to families should be explicit.

There are numerous models of separated families splitting financial responsibilities to a school. When separated parents have amicable arrangements for the schooling of their children, the financial arrangements are often easily negotiated with the school. Models may include a 50/50 split of all school expenses. Any number of various percentages of shared responsibility can work for separated parents and schools. When parents can't agree, or one parent can't fulfil their agreed obligations, it gets tricky for school leaders.

Once separated parents come to individual agreements with the school for their financial obligations, which ultimately have to be agreed upon by both parents in most cases, the school principal can treat each parent as separate cases to manage. When the parents can't agree on arrangements and/or one parent refuses to engage in the process of negotiation for financial responsibilities, then we have a dilemma.

As the world evolves and time moves on, models of families also evolve. There is more variety of family models than ever before. In schools it is common for families to enrol in a school where they believe like-minded families will be present. With the diversity of family models, acceptance of difference is important for any school to be inclusive and welcoming.

Some schools, especially those founded in faith-based traditions, may have parents with conservative views of what constitutes a family. Same-sex parents in traditional schools may face a variety of receptions, from some who welcome them as any other parent to others who may ostracise them as representing a family model they object to. Same-sex parents are a legitimate family model, yet there are some faith-based communities that cannot publicly acknowledge these families. The best they can do is welcome families, as they do all families. For example, the welcome may be in a small gathering with the school leaders, who may be reluctant to make any public acknowledgement of the family as it may contravene their church teachings. This is a legitimate moral dilemma for school leaders where their evolving private beliefs might be at odds with the traditional views of the church. Private beliefs of individuals often evolve more quickly than those of church structures.

Family models also include people who choose to have families on their own, whether through adoption, surrogacy or artificial insemination. Some of these families may be hard for some fellow parents to understand and accept. Divorced parents were once treated in a similar way; however, acceptance of divorced parents is now common, and hopefully acceptance of all family models will be the norm soon.

Families where one or both parents are incarcerated or in rehabilitation programs may also find acceptance within school communities difficult. Often these parents are "hidden", with their absence explained through creative writing. How a parent who has served time is welcomed back into the school community may very much depend on the example set by school leaders and parent leaders. If the principal is seen to be welcoming of the parent, that will go a long way towards the community accepting them.

It is in meeting these families, *all* families, and welcoming them to a school community that school leaders show humanity in building positive relationships while accepting the limitations of the accepted protocols. It takes a courageous leader to do this. It is well worth doing.

Scenarios to Consider

Scenario 1

Context: The child of a separated couple is injured at school. The parent with custody is not answering their phone and hence can't be contacted to collect the child. The second parent refuses to collect the child, reminding the school staff that the non-contactable parent is responsible for the child's welfare on their custody days. The school is following the court orders as is the non-custodial parent.

Dilemma: How do the school staff provide the necessary care for the student when the parents can't or won't assist in a time of need?

Options: A legitimate medical emergency may require the principal to plead with the non-custodial parent to attend to the child's needs. Alternately, there may be emergency contacts on the custodial parent's side that could be the next person to care for the child. As an extreme solution, the school staff may have to take the child to medical care or call an ambulance to attend to the child.

Whatever the course of action, messages must be left with the parents so that when they do get the message, they are aware of the school's caring actions. The welfare of the student must be the primary concern and priority on occasions such as these. If the five P's need to be bent or broken to ensure the health and wellbeing of the child, the school leader is assuming responsibility for the student in place of the parents.

Scenario 2

Context: A family needs to adjust their financial responsibilities to the school as a result of their separation. The courts have been vague in their instructions regarding the split of school financial responsibilities, which have allowed for each parent's solicitors to interpret the instructions to their benefit. (Sadly this happens.) One parent refuses to enter into dialogue with the school or their previous partner to negotiate a change in the financial arrangements for the school. The principal knows that the parent who has engaged with the school to negotiate their portion of school expenses can't afford their portion.

The principal has engaged with the unfinancial parent to negotiate a reasonable portion of the outstanding debt, knowing they have limited capacity to meet these obligations. The second parent is reluctant to engage, believing their contribution to child support covers all school fees, which should be paid by the unfinancial parent. The child is due to go on school camp, which is an additional expense. The unfinancial parent offers to pay a portion of camp expenses in lieu of their portion of school fees for the term.

Dilemma: Should the principal accept the unfinancial parent's contribution to the camp and forgo the school fees for the term? Should the principal attempt to engage with the other parent and ask for camp fees, believing that parent can afford the camp fees?

Options: The principal could deny the student from attending the camp as the parents can't afford the experience. The remaining school expenses – including school fees, books, resources, excursions, uniforms and computers – need to be negotiated in a fair manner. If solicitors are involved, explicit instructions are key. If solicitors are not involved, the school principal may be required to negotiate how best to retrieve school expenses.

Most schools can afford to "carry" a small number of student expenses, so the child could attend the camp and the principal could then determine how the expenses can be covered even in part. To retrieve the more significant school expenses the principal may put suggestions of a financial plan in writing to both parents. The instructions can remain confidential from each parent if they have separated and want their finances kept private.

If the principal wishes to follow the five P's, they may choose to engage with debt collectors to retrieve the funds. This may jeopardise the relationships and may not retrieve funds. Debt collectors do send clear messages to the families in debt, but attempts to keep relationships with the families are important. Guiding families to fulfil their financial obligations is an unpalatable part of leading schools, yet it has to be done.

Scenario 3

Context: A family, relatively new to the school, has broken the pick-up procedures by insisting that a teacher opens the driveway gate to allow them to exit. The gate has been closed for the safe exodus of many students before the students depart. This family is unaware of the school protocols, and they believe they have exceptional reasons to use the particular driveway in question. The teacher on duty at the time explains to the parents that the gate cannot be opened because "that is the rule".

While the parent is distressed at the teacher's response, they do understand the protocols designed to keep everybody safe. The parent then chooses to inform the principal that the teacher's conduct was less than accommodating and, in the words of the parents, "quite rude". The teacher was correct in insisting that the protocols be followed for the safety of all the students, but the parent believes they had exceptional reasons to bend the protocols. The principal wasn't there and was given the feedback by the parent.

Dilemma: Should the principal believe the parent's recount that the teacher was rude and failed to accommodate the family? Or should they support the teacher's practice in enforcing the rules in what the teacher believes was a professional and efficient manner? How can the principal build relationships with families in their school if they're not accommodating exceptional stories yet be seen to be supporting the teachers?

Options: On this occasion the principal could first go to the teacher to seek their information and their recount of the events in question. The principal should reserve their judgement until hearing the teacher's version of events. The principal could then ask the teacher if there would be any exceptional circumstances in which they would consider opening the gate to allow a parent to exit, even though it would be going against school protocols? If the teacher insists that the rules are made to be followed and there are no exceptions as to why the gate may be opened, this would indicate the rigid nature of the teacher.

We don't live in a world of black and white; we live in a world that is very grey, where exceptions need to be made on occasions. And on this occasion, by being adamant that the school rules have to be followed for the safety of other children, the teacher might have jeopardised future enrolments and may have clouded that parent's opinion about the school. Do the protocols on this occasion outweigh the opportunity to build relationships?

When exploring the scenario further it may become apparent that there were very few other children about and that it was perfectly safe to allow that particular family to exit the car park without threatening the welfare and wellbeing of any other students. It may also become apparent that the teacher was firm in their belief that there were no exceptions as to how that particular school rule should be enforced. On this occasion protocols could be bent to build relationships as the safety aspect was not relevant. When addressing the issue with the teacher, it is important that this done relatively privately so the teacher is not advised as to alternative behaviour in front of a group of people.

Scenario 4

Context: A student wears a symbol of their religion or culture to school, which is in breach of the school uniform policy. The student is in a minority group within the school demographics. The school promotes itself as being a welcoming and inclusive school with high standards. The school principal wishes to uphold the school mission and vision to be welcoming and inclusive while maintaining high standards.

Dilemma: Conscious of the diversity that exists in society and wishing to keep the support of the school board and staff, how does the principal keep high, consistent standards while recognising, accepting and welcoming difference and the freedom for a degree of self-expression?

Options: The principal might seek the opinions of the leadership team to gauge their thoughts on building relationships within the protocols. Following this, the principal may share their thoughts on the same topic before making a decision. Certain symbols of religious or cultural significance may be permitted if worn subtly or if they are recognised as an identifying feature. If the symbol was to jeopardise any workplace and health standards, the student may be asked to remove it on safety grounds.

It is highly probable that not all staff, nor all parents, will agree to accept breaking the five P's to build relationships. That is the joy of leadership. Not everyone will agree with decisions, however transparency goes a long way for group acceptance of hard decisions.

Scenario 5

Context: A student is expected to have parental permission to participate in school swimming lessons, which start today. The parent who has custody of the child for the current week has not signed the form and cannot be contacted for approval. The other parent refuses to give permission, possibly in an act of spite or to teach the other parent a lesson. As the school requires written approval from at least one parent of the student to allow participation in swimming, the missing signature creates a dilemma.

Dilemma: To deny the student a swimming lesson over the parents' failure to provide permission seems to punish the child. What are the staff risking by allowing the child to participate? Based on previous knowledge and experience, does the risk outweigh breaking the five P's, or is allowing the child to participate building the relationship with the family and student? Does breaching the five P's render the school expectations irrelevant? Should the school allow the child to participate as they have the required clothing though not the signed permission form? Understanding that the parents have paid for the swimming lessons and the child is ready to participate, should the school staff give permission or stand firm on the protocols and deny the child the swimming lesson?

Options: The risk is minimal that any harm would come to the child by participating. The school principal could authorise the student's participation in the swimming lesson and contact the parent explaining their decision.

Alternately, the principal could uphold the need for signed permission form and send a clear message to the parents that the school has protocols that must be followed. What message are they sending to the parents? The five P's are important and the school has standards and expectations that should be upheld.

Scenario 6

Context: A teacher has communicated the schedule for parent-teacher interviews and separated parents have booked two separate appointments, adding to the teacher's workload. The separated parents have new partners and would prefer their partners attend the parent-teacher interview as they are involved in the upbringing of the children when in their care. Each parent would prefer to have separate parent-teacher interviews for their child.

Dilemma: Does the teacher (or school leadership team) insist that parents have one interview per child? If the separated parents can't agree to both attending the one interview, they may have to determine which parent attends. How should the teacher handle that situation? Does the school have practices, protocols, procedures, processes and policies in place for this modelling?

Options: To build relationships the teacher may offer separate interviews, while limiting the attendance to the birth parents only. This would allow space for each parent while adding pressure to the teacher to repeat the same feedback to each parent, but it does risk the relationship with the significant carer (step-parent) who may be responsible for the supervision, support and care of the child.

Alternately, the teacher could offer one interview and ask both parents to attend, which they may do reluctantly. This does risk jeopardising the peacefulness of the relationship between the separated parents by forcing them to be in the same room. School leaders also need to be aware of any court orders preventing the parents from attending meetings together. In the case of family violence situations, there may be court orders instructing a safe distance between each party. School leaders must follow these instructions.

Summary

School staff must provide a safe environment for everyone who visits, works or learns on their school site. Rules are necessary for people to know the expectations for complying to the five P's to provide a safe environment. Within each school, the relationships formed will go a long way to providing a high-performing school. Teachers, leaders and parents must work together so the students are the beneficiaries of the collective work of their caring adults. When the rules inhibit positive relationships, a leaders' judgement will guide the community through change.

As schools function within a culture that relies on harmonious relationships, it is essential that the rules promote relationships and that relationships exist contentedly within the rules. There needs to be a balance between prioritising the relationships and the rules. Both need to co-exist. It is not a case of either/or, it is about balancing both.

"Clarity is kindness."

Melinda Ross, Primary Learning Leader,
St Columba's School, Wilston

Think of your own SCHOOL RULES and PARENT RELATIONSHIPS scenario and do a response analysis

Scenario:

Dilemma:

Options:

Response checklist:

- ☑ **Does the response improve the learning and wellbeing of students, staff and families?**
- ☑ **Workplace health and safety**: Will the action keep people safe?
- ☑ **Transparency**: Do stakeholders understand the rationale for the action?
- ☑ **Best interests of the majority**: Is the action in the best interests of the majority of stakeholders?
- ☑ **Fairness**: Does the action meet the needs of stakeholders?
- ☑ **Practicality and sustainability**: Can the action be done and continue to be done?
- ☑ **Cost-benefit analysis**: Does the cost of the action warrant the outcome?
- ☑ **Legal requirements**: Does the action meet the obligations of relevant legislation?

Chapter 7

SELECTION OF SCHOOL REPRESENTATIVES

One of the most emotive issues in school life for parents can be any real or perceived injustice which is thought to impact their child. The selection of children to represent the school is an honour and a privilege and often the result of hard work. If a child is to be selected to represent the school, there needs to be transparent criteria to justify their selection. However, on occasions there may be reasons to go outside the selection criteria and select a child for a particular event. This chapter unpacks how it's possible to balance the criteria for school selection with a certain latitude available to families in exceptional circumstances.

The Australian movie *The Merger* is about a fictious country town where refugees are settled. The local Australian Football League (AFL) team is on verge of closing or merging until a former player, an outcast in the town for being a Greenie and closing the mill (a major business in the town), invites refugees and locals to play for the AFL team. He also agrees to coach the team.

The team's best player has a tendency to make racist comments to one player in particular, who is a refugee. The team coach selected the best player to play in the semi-final, as picking the best team meant a better opportunity for wining. It means that a dedicated, regular player has to miss out on playing the final.

The coach has a change of heart and mind on the advice of the club president and omits the best player for the final. He drops the racist player and selects an average player to play in the grand final. The story concludes with the average player kicking the winning goal.

The Merger highlights how sporting selections can be based purely on ability and by following strict criteria. This approach may be the choice selectors make if wining at all costs is the priority. If participation and participants' attitudes are priorities, then building relationships may be of greater value.

Selection for school representative honours is a proud achievement for students. Whether it is on the sporting arena or in the musical sphere, or whether it involves artistic talents that can be displayed elsewhere, any opportunity for a child to represent their school should be acknowledged and supported. When it comes to selecting students for representative honours, school staff are often left with the task of making the process fair and transparent and being faithful to the process which acknowledges the student's hard work. Let's address each sphere separately.

Sporting Selections

In the sporting arena it is quite common that are qualifying standards which students would have to meet to represent the school. There may also be opportunities for students to represent the school in non-competitive sporting events which are basically based on participation. Students may be selected in recognition of their commitment to attend training, effectively putting in the hard work. Parents are often very aware of their own children's sporting ability and will have an opinion as to whether or not their child should be selected to represent the school, particularly if qualifying standards need to be met or if they believe the student has a higher skill level than other students selected.

Schools need to have a very transparent process by which they can select students for representative honours. Any failure to disclose the transparent process, qualifying standards or selection criteria is fraught with parents challenging the school's practices and processes and leaving them open to question how students may be selected. Competitive parents may seek exemptions or concessions when it comes to having their children selected for teams.

Analysing the process and following the process as prescribed may mean that relationships are harmed or jeopardised when parents or students feel they are not given the opportunity to perform or that they are better than those selected. Are the teachers seen to be building a relationship with the selected students? School staff may also have to justify selections to students who miss out who believe they are more skilled or who believe their results warrant selection over students who were selected on historical performances.

In some independent colleges and high schools around the country it is not uncommon that students are "ordained" from a very young age to be selected in the top teams throughout their schooling. School staff need to be very cautious about promoting students from a very young age or ordaining them to greatness when circumstances may change in the following years. School sport and school selections can be political and emotional. Hence transparency is the biggest ally for school leaders when the emotion of the school selection process overrides calm conversations. If transparency is upheld, then building relationships is possible. If the process is compromised or altered in favour of relationships, in favour of keeping parents happy or in favour of keeping students or staff happy, relationships can be eroded very quickly.

Artistic Pursuits

When it comes time for the selection of representatives for musical pursuits, whether choir or band performances, there may not be qualifying standards or levels to be met for the students to represent the school. Students may simply enjoy singing and hence be a part of the school choir and will represent the school at eisteddfods or other performances. Some children may in fact not be very good singers. How does the choir teacher build a relationship with those students without shattering their love and enjoyment of musical pursuits? This is a great challenge for staff who manage activities that are participation based and not necessarily skills based.

However, when it comes to representative honours where a school wants the best performers to represent the school, teachers need to have diplomatic ways to explain to students there may be other opportunities or there may be activities for which they are more suited without shattering their self-esteem. If the teacher wants the best musical performers to sing and play at concerts, eisteddfods or public gatherings, they need to be honest with the students who are there for a love of music but with minimal ability. This is a case where teachers need to act in the best interests of the group while being honest with students. They need diplomatically tell the students that there may be other opportunities for them to represent the school or participate in activities but this particular endeavour may not be their forte.

Schools have many opportunities to publicly display their students' work in all manner of cultural pursuits. Teachers with a passion for a particular area may be able to provide students the opportunity to display their work in a variety of public settings. If there are no qualifying criteria which a child must meet to represent their school, some cultural pursuits will welcome participation at all levels. These opportunities give students the chance to showcase their talents in a public setting without being concerned about meeting certain criteria or being super competitive. It also allows the teacher to place more emphasis on participation than on performance and competitiveness. Is winning everything? For some students, teachers and parents it might be. Does winning at all costs outweigh the relationships between teachers, students and parents? There are many questions as to how school leaders find balance in such scenarios.

Competitiveness

Each school will have their own philosophy about the degree of competitiveness they wish to promote as a cultural trait of their school. Some schools are known for being super competitive in all manner of pursuits. It could be the chess club. It could be STEM – science technology engineering and maths – activities. It could be brilliant musical performances or choir recitals. It could be outstanding academic achievements through things like NAPLAN results or Optiminds performances. It could be brilliant sporting achievements.

Schools have a lot of choice in how they provide their students with opportunities to showcase their talents beyond the school. Schools need to promote the culture which they wish to be known for within their communities. If a school promotes a culture of participation and high levels of student engagement, some parents will be attracted to that model. If a school is focused on the pursuit of excellence and high-achieving brilliance in all activities or a specific activity, such as academic, sporting musical or other pursuits, that's what they may become known for and that will attract some families. Schools are often environments of like-minded families with like-minded philosophies. It is when philosophies within the parent body or within the staff body clash that conflict may arise.

As teachers it's not uncommon that we acknowledge and reward students for simply participating. This must cease so that we can affirm students' efforts and we can affirm improvement and performance not participation. Students should not be praised for getting out of bed and turning up to school. It is common that students receive participation awards for simply arriving and engaging in an activity. This does not give them any motivation to do their best and strive to improve. Not only that, it also diminishes the value of getting any recognition, as students do not have to try to be rewarded.

Former American educator Rita Pierson (RIP) spoke in a TED talk about how she responded to a student who only achieved two marks out of 20 in a maths test. She drew a big smiley face and wrote "+2". The student asked Pierson, "Is this an F?", and she said "Yes, it's an F." The student asked, "Why then did I get a smiley face and a +2?", to which Pierson replied, "Because you didn't miss them all and you're on the way". Her response gave the student some encouragement, a growth mindset and a sense of optimism.

American psychologist Carol Dweck promotes a growth mindset for all students and all people. We need to reward students for effort as well as achievement. And when we have selection criteria we must be transparent so that students are aware of what they can do to improve and what they can do to meet a standard if they want to represent their school.

Scenarios to Consider

Scenario 1

Context: A student is away for the selection trials of their school's sporting team. Their parent believes the child is highly skilled and that playing for a club team at a high level should be evidence enough of their suitability to make the team. The school followed its selection policy and only selected students who attended the trials. The parents of the student believe their child is more skilled than students who attended the trials and were selected.

Dilemma: Where students who have proven their ability and met qualifying standards in an external environment seek selection, should that be taken into account when teachers are making selections? Should the school leaders make exceptions and include the student who was absent from the trials? Should the school leaders make exceptions when students will be fit and able to play at the time of the carnival or event but missed the selection trials due to injury? Should they be allowed to play?

Options: The school leaders need to explain the selection criteria to the parents before the selection of school teams. The staff will have selection criteria, time frames for trials and selections, and the details of any school commitments related to selection for the school team. Staff should be encouraged to share this process with the students and families for transparency. This transparency minimises the opportunity for parents to question selections. If exceptions to the five P's are permissible, staff should elaborate on that variation for all relevant parents and staff.

When parents do question selections (and they will), staff need to be calm, clear and concise in delivering the message of the five P's. They may also choose to restate the school's philosophy on the value of participation over the emphasis on high performance and winning. School leaders and teachers need to be consistent in their message and transparent in their process.

Scenario 2

Context: Historically a school has participated in a sports competition on a weekend that is supervised by school staff. This year no school staff are available to attend the carnival and supervise students. However, a group of enthusiastic parents are willing to train and manage the students and supervise and organise them at the carnival. The school sports coordinator is content to not enter the students for the carnival this year and seeks the principal's support of the decision. Expecting some feedback from the parents, the sports coordinator briefs the principal and gets prepared to respond to any vocal, disappointed parents.

As expected, a few parents contact the school and express their disappointment at the decision to not enter students in the carnival. The parents ask the principal to reconsider the decision. The sports coordinator doesn't want to change the decision and is concerned that it is a poor reflection on his work. The principal commits to listening to the parents but won't make any decision without further discussion with the sports coordinator.

Dilemma: The principal wants to encourage parent participation in the life of the school. The parents wish to support the school and offer their time and energy to provide opportunities for their children and ease pressure on the staff. Ultimately it is good to provide opportunities for students. How can the principal support the sports coordinator and build their professional relationship while working within protocols (workplace health and safety; public liability insurance) and honouring the historical involvement that some students are keen to replicate with the support of their parents?

Options: The principal could just shut down any discussion and not listen to parents nor explore options. Or the principal could ask for any other staff volunteers to lead the participation. The principal should check with WHS officer what is legally acceptable for discharging school responsibility to parents.

There are more issues in this scenario. Should staff be made to work on the weekend? If no staff are available to attend the carnival and parents understand that the school can't discharge their responsibility to parents, then the school may not enter teams on this occasion. This approach supports the sports coordinator and honours the parents' interest. While it is disappointing for students not to participate, it is a good lesson for all that circumstances change and that there are strict protocols within which schools have to operate. It is possible to build relationships with the sports coordinator and parents while being faithful to the limitations of protocols.

If staff are available, it is possible to follow protocols, involve the parents and provide a good experience for the students. This will build relationships with parents, ease the pressure on the sports coordinator and act within the protocols. Changing events that have historically happened in schools is always fraught with backlash. Principals beware!

Summary

Opportunities for students to represent their school is a privilege and something they should work hard towards. Whether the opportunity for school representation is in the sporting arena, musical and creative pursuits or academic challenges, schools must build relationships with students and their parents to ensure the school is honoured. There needs to be transparency for all involved and an acceptance of the role each stakeholder plays.

"We have cultivated a positive and orderly learning environment where teachers come to teach and students come to learn."

Mark Harris, Principal,
Auburn North Public School

Think of your own SELECTION OF SCHOOL REPRESENTATIVES scenario and do a response analysis

Scenario:

Dilemma:

Options:

Response checklist:
- ☑ **Does the response improve the learning and wellbeing of students, staff and families?**
- ☑ **Workplace health and safety**: Will the action keep people safe?
- ☑ **Transparency**: Do stakeholders understand the rationale for the action?
- ☑ **Best interests of the majority**: Is the action in the best interests of the majority of stakeholders?
- ☑ **Fairness**: Does the action meet the needs of stakeholders?
- ☑ **Practicality and sustainability**: Can the action be done and continue to be done?
- ☑ **Cost-benefit analysis**: Does the cost of the action warrant the outcome?
- ☑ **Legal requirements**: Does the action meet the obligations of relevant legislation?

Chapter 8
BEHAVIOUR MANAGEMENT

The expectations of student behaviour in a school should be consistent across ages and gender. However, when school leaders and teachers accept difference in school communities, should behavioural expectations vary? This chapter unpacks how processes, practices, protocols, procedures and policies can be in place to ensure transparency in behaviour management structures within a school while accepting and acknowledging difference.

There are occasions where unique qualities and unique individuals may be given more latitude than others with a justified rationale. Schools need, want and value consistency for parents, staff and students. So when a school leader or a teacher deviates from a consistent approach that is accepted and understood by the school community this can create tension. This chapter explores how it's possible to build relationships within those protocols, with transparency being a key factor.

> The movie *Wonder* is the story of August Pullman, better known as Auggie. Auggie, a boy with a rare facial abnormality, enters the fifth grade in a private school where he befriends Jack. The two form a strong bond while facing the bullies in their class. Throughout the movie relationships are challenged and protocols are tested among students, parents and staff.

On one such occasion Jack defends Auggie from a peer who has been mean to Auggie. Jack and the protagonist end up in a wrestle and have to be separated by a teacher. The subsequent trip to the principal's office results in both boys being suspended. During his talk to Jack, Principal Tushman acknowledges that standing up for a mate is the honourable thing to do, especially when your mate is marginalised. However, the school and principal believe physical aggression cannot be tolerated and hence there has to be a consequence.

Auggie's popularity and circle of friends grows over the year, but he is still bullied by Julian and his friends until a teacher, Mr Browne, notices. The principal confronts Julian and his parents with evidence, including hate notes and a class picture with Auggie photoshopped out. Julian's mother admits she deleted Auggie from the picture, defends Julian's actions and insists students should not be exposed to Auggie. Despite her threats to pull funding, Julian is suspended for two days, forcing him to miss a nature retreat. As they leave, Julian's mum declares he will not be back in the fall and Julian apologises.

School leaders regularly face similar dilemmas when disciplining students for poor choices. Understanding the backstory to a specific altercation may allow the school leader to act with compassion and understanding. Yet this may cause some disharmony if the school rules and consequences are not followed or enforced consistently and rigidly. How do school leaders balance building positive relationships within the protocols in such scenarios? Should there be unquestioned consistency? Or should exceptions be allowed, and if so, under what criteria? Who gets to decide? Who should be informed?

Expectations

If we consider a school as a microcosm of society, then schools certainly have laws that are designed and introduced to keep people safe. Staff, students, visitors, parents, families and guests all have a right to feel safe. What happens, though, when those laws are broken? What happens when the safety and welfare of students are jeopardised through the inappropriate behaviour of fellow students, staff or parents?

Ultimately it is the school leader's responsibility to ensure the safety of all people within the school community. It is also the responsibility of the school leader to build relationships, because it is only through a culture of trust and collaboration that children will learn. If a child threatens the harmonious relationships within a community, the school leader has to then balance building relationships while following the five P's.

Creating a safe environment is one of the key roles of a class teacher. A safe environment means the environment is free of hazards that may jeopardise learning, with a positive emotional and learning space created by a culture of trust and collaboration within the class. All students have the right to feel safe. All students have the right to a high-quality education. The *Alice Springs (Mparntwe) Education Declaration* (2020) stresses that that everyone should have every right to a high-quality education. If a student's behaviour jeopardises the safety of themselves or others, the opportunity for learning is threatened, and teachers need to have strategies by which all children can learn. It is quite common in schools, particularly primary schools, that teachers negotiate with their students a "class covenant" or a class set of rules. They may also be in a position to negotiate with the students the consequences for breaches of the class rules. Ideally teachers will have affirming strategies that children will strive to achieve to get rewards for good behaviour.

However, there is also often the need for teachers, and certainly school leaders, to impose consequences for misbehaviour. It is quite common for schools to develop behaviour support plans, which should be promoted and known throughout the school community so that when students do misbehave or make poor choices they are well aware of the consequences they'll be facing. Certainly in high schools those consequences are well known and understood by the students. In primary schools it may be more difficult to explain to a 4- or 5-year-old that if they behave in a certain way the consequence will be this. Children often react spontaneously and impulsively and hence won't think through the consequences for their behaviour, good or bad. As they mature they may be in a position to understand that all behaviours have a consequence.

As Hattie (2008) says, it is critical that teachers "know thy students". Apart from students' academic ability, teachers need to know their backgrounds, personalities, strengths and learning styles. There are many pieces of the puzzle that are critical for teachers to know and understand so that when a student's behaviour varies from their normal behaviour, or even if a student's behaviour is frequently outside the school's expectations, they may understand why the student is responding in a particular way.

It is human nature to behave in a certain way to either access or avoid something. Students may misbehave because they find the work too difficult (to avoid work and access attention). They may also misbehave because the work is too easy and not challenging enough to activate their grey matter (to access harder work). If a teacher understands their students, especially when the students misbehave, they can then respond with a considered position.

Consequences

If a child's behaviour is so extreme that the school leaders choose to follow the most extreme course of action – that is, expelling a child from their school – they will justify that by saying they need to keep their school community members safe. They may also rationalise such behaviour by saying that the child needs a fresh start and a new community. It does beg the question as to how relationships within that community can be reconciled if they are broken when the wrongdoer is removed from the community? How are relationships to be fostered and promoted if a member who broke the relationship is removed from the situation?

Certainly in society when people commit serious crimes and rehabilitation seems unlikely then locking them up and throwing away the key is often the accepted course of action. Still the position of judges who have the task of sentencing serious criminals isn't an enviable one. They need to follow the five P's. Judges follow precedents in most cases (a possible sixth P). They need to be seen to be keeping society safe. They also need to be seen to give the perpetrator an opportunity for rehabilitation. Similarly in schools when students misbehave school leaders have the opportunity to use that as a chance to educate and to teach as opposed to punishing them.

When a child's behaviour warrants a consequence from a school leader, the leader has to determine the rationale for that consequence. Is the consequence purely being administered as a punitive response, as in a punishment which is designed to admonish the student; or is the consequence designed as a disciplinary action by which the student may learn through restorative practices? The school must also understand that public consequences send a message to more than just the student and their family involved. Consequences that are made public also send a message to families of other students and to the staff. This can prove to be a very strategic practice that allows school leaders to send clear messages as to their expectations regarding student behaviour.

Deviation from Agreed Protocols

When a child misbehaves and requires a significant consequence, are the protocols followed without question, or do the context and the individual affect the action taken by the school leadership team?

The more rules schools have, the more difficult it is for them to be implemented consistently. The bigger the school, the more variables there are by virtue of the number of people – that's human nature. It is probably preferable that schools have a few overarching expectations that students, staff and families understand that also allow some degree of latitude when working with the greatest variable, which is the student.

Primary schools often have rules such as "treat everyone with respect", "keep your hands and feet to yourself", "one person speaks at a time", "treat others as you would like to be treated", "stay safe" and "be inclusive". These overarching philosophies demonstrate the teacher's expectations as to what behaviours they expect from students. Ideally teachers working at the same school will have the same philosophy and similar expectations on students' behaviour. However, when teachers have a different interpretation as to what is acceptable behaviour, schools may end up with some conflict.

As new teachers arrive at school, ideally they will have a similar philosophy to their colleagues. As new school leaders arrive, they are likely to follow historical expectations that have been in place. This is a question that school leaders face every time they change schools. Do they impose their value system and their expectations on the community when in fact the community may have longstanding historical expectations that are accepted and known by the community? Some school leaders will have their own favourite expectations that may challenge some existing philosophies. The dilemma for school leaders is about building the relationships within the communities while having clear processes, practices, policies, procedures and protocols which the community will understand and allowing the school leader to set their own theme for the school. Once again this is a balancing act for the school leaders. A school leader may be passionate about all staff wearing hats on playground duty. A school leader may be passionate about keeping the school grounds clean and tidy and their classrooms clean and tidy, yet if a teacher does not follow that same degree of emphasis on that particular practice, how does a school leader then create a culture of harmony and trust? It is the school leader's position to set the standards and set the tone for the school.

There is a common saying that the standard we walk past is the standard we accept. If a teacher or a school leader walks past rubbish on the playground and doesn't do anything about it, they're accepting that standard for their school. Having said that, it could be argued that a little piece of rubbish in the playground does not affect the teaching and learning aspect that the school is mandated to implement. This is true in some cases. However, it does create a culture of socially acceptable high standards.

When a teacher refuses to follow the school expectations regarding wearing of hats while on playground duty in favour of invisible sunscreen, it may be difficult for the principal to challenge that teacher without some degree of pushback. Does a teacher wearing a hat on playground duty make or break the academic improvement of those students? No. And yet it does set a cultural tone within the school if the teacher cannot be seen as a good role model. Teachers' behaviour and living out appropriate behaviours, both in the school and beyond the school, is so important because teachers, whether they like it or not, are role models for their students and public figures.

Teachers and school leaders need to be aware that social media can be one of the greatest friends and one of the greatest risks, because there are no secrets in today's society, with much of our lives accessible via social media. For teachers and school leaders, a word of warning: be very cautious about what you post on social media while you're in the teaching profession. It may come back to bite you. Parents and employers can learn a lot about staff, even before they have arrived in the community, just by viewing social media platforms – and they do!

Duty Rosters

Managing duty rosters for staff can be a challenge when there are protocols which describe certain hours of duty within which people must work. Working beyond the prescribed hours may present some issues. School staff need to keep children safe, in which case we may have to balance relationships and keep people happy (or at least content) while working within the protocols.

In some school environments there are industrial agreements within which schools operate. Hours of duty for staff are explicitly explained in any enterprise bargaining agreement. One of the caveats around such agreements includes the statement that references the need to provide a safe environment for the students. If a teacher is expected to work a minimum of 30 hours a week including playground duties, planning meetings and face-to-face teaching, yet the school leader cannot guarantee the safety of the students without asking the teachers to work longer than the 30 hours (even with the additional hour that some agreements allow), what is the school leader to do? Is the safety of the students a higher priority than the welfare of the staff, who may be overworked? Does the school leader only approach those willing, hard-working staff to do additional duties because they understand that's a necessary behaviour and practice to keep the students safe? Or does the school leader impose additional responsibilities for all teaching staff to ensure the safety of the students, accepting that there will be some pushback?

This is the balancing act between choosing to create positive harmonious relationships while having practices that ensure the safety of all. It is not uncommon for school leaders to take on additional responsibilities and duties in the playground just to keep the peace and so that the teachers are working within their hours of duty. Some may say this is an act of good leadership by which the leaders are looking after the staff, while also ensuring a safe environment for the students. It does create a tension for school leaders, who also have the right to feel safe and to have their welfare managed. Tension is created when the provision for staff is not high enough to provide a safe environment at all times without some staff working in excess of the agreed work hours. The teaching profession works well above and beyond the hours for which they are paid – that is largely acknowledged and widely accepted within society. However, it is becoming more common in conversations that the welfare of teachers needs to be managed so that they can provide high-quality education for all students and we can have high-performing schools. If teachers are continually asked to work above and beyond, that is not a sustainable or realistic model. Remember the key question: is what we are doing improving the learning and wellbeing of students, staff and families?

Scenarios to Consider

Scenario 1

Context: A student with significant learning and social needs (multiple diagnoses) is reluctant to wear the mandatory school shoes. There does not appear to be any physical reason why the student should have to wear bright coloured shoes in lieu of mandatory black shoes. Some staff are reluctant to accept this blatant disregard for the school rules and want a serious sanction imposed on the student. There is more to this real-life story. The student's single mother has been battling to get the student to take his medication and has a daily struggle to get him to school. Is wearing the correct school shoes a higher priority?

Dilemma: The principal needs to uphold the standards of the school, while showing leadership in understanding the struggles families with students with diverse needs have on a daily basis. Should the principal allow the student to wear the colourful shoes to school or insist he wears the mandated shoes? And how much information should the principal share with the staff, some of whom may have difficulty with the student's attitude and demeanour?

Options: The principal, who understands the student's needs and family situation, may need to share enough information with the staff for them to understand the rationale behind the decision to allow the student to wear the incorrect footwear.

The principal may also take the opportunity to instruct the student that there is a limit to breaching the school rules. As the child prepares to enter high school, where there is likely to be less acceptance of diversity by breaching school rules, the safe environment of a primary school can be the training ground for conformity where possible and necessary. Such an explanation may also serve the mother well, as working hand in hand may allow the student to make progress in following school rules that are essential for safety and learning.

Wearing the correct uniform is important for many schools. If there are valid reasons why a student may not wear the correct uniform, then some degree of flexibility is relevant.

Scenario 2

Context: A student is being disruptive during class by engaging with other students and preventing them from working. The student is also looking up websites that are not related to the classwork. When corrected by the teacher, the student swears under his breath yet audible enough for the students and staff to hear it. The teacher immediately calls for the deputy principal and wants the student suspended.

Dilemma: How can the deputy principal be seen to enforce the protocols of the school's behaviour expectations while understanding the student's behaviour? Does it matter that the student has significant stress in their life, external to school? Does it matter that the student wasn't directing their frustration at anyone, rather just frustrated with the circumstances? Does it matter that the student can't do the work and hence may act out to avoid the work? Yes, yes and yes – all of these contextual questions are relevant.

Options: The deputy can withdraw the student, call his parents and send him home, as his behaviour, on face value, is completely unacceptable. The deputy could discuss with the student the reasons behind their behaviour, knowing that student's behaviour is to access or avoid something. The deputy can explain to the student that school rules are in place to ensure the school is a safe place for teachers to teach and students to learn. Any behaviour that threatens that environment needs to be checked, and consequences are necessary for the student and for the school members so everyone knows that the rules will be enforced.

The deputy could negotiate consequences for the student that illustrate behavioural expectations while accepting his rationale for the behaviour. The deputy could inform the student's parents of the behaviour in question and seek their support for the consequences.

Summary

Consistency of practice when managing student behaviour is one value that schools appreciate. Knowing that there will be consequences for good behaviour (affirmations) and for inappropriate behaviour (disciplines) provides confidence within the staff, parents and student groups. Yet there is no one-size-fits-all solution, and every child has unique reasons for their behaviour. School leaders and teachers need great wisdom to navigate through the five P's of behaviour management while building positive, harmonious relationships. There needs to be a balance between enforcing the behaviour management expectations of the school and exercising discretion when exceptions may be made to build relationships.

"What is essential for some is beneficial for all."

Melinda Ross, Primary Learning Leader,
St Columba's Primary School, Wilston

Think of your own BEHAVIOUR MANAGEMENT scenario and do a response analysis

Scenario:

Dilemma:

Options:

Response checklist:

- ☑ **Does the response improve the learning and wellbeing of students, staff and families?**
- ☑ **Workplace health and safety**: Will the action keep people safe?
- ☑ **Transparency**: Do stakeholders understand the rationale for the action?
- ☑ **Best interests of the majority**: Is the action in the best interests of the majority of stakeholders?
- ☑ **Fairness**: Does the action meet the needs of stakeholders?
- ☑ **Practicality and sustainability**: Can the action be done and continue to be done?
- ☑ **Cost-benefit analysis**: Does the cost of the action warrant the outcome?
- ☑ **Legal requirements**: Does the action meet the obligations of relevant legislation?

Chapter 9
CULTURAL DIVERSITY

Schools are microcosms of society, with most schools having significant cultural diversity within the student population and often within the staff. Cultural awareness has a greater profile now than in the past, when schools had fewer students and staff with different cultural backgrounds. Nowadays it is common for schools to have students and staff with diverse cultural backgrounds, whether they were born overseas or their parents were born overseas. Each culture has its own unique customs and traditions. Schools may choose to celebrate cultural diversity with activities like multicultural days where the school celebrates the cultural diversity within their community. This chapter unpacks some of the five P's that schools need to work within to build understanding, acceptance and inclusion while honouring the customs and traditions of different cultures.

The First Nations People of Australia have been mistreated for hundreds of years and continue to be mistreated by some members of our society today. As a result of the apology by the then Prime Minister Kevin Rudd in 2008, processes, practices, procedures, protocols and policies were established to help ensure First Nations People are afforded the recognition and respect that all humans deserve. This chapter explores how balancing the five P's with building positive relationships is relevant to First Nations People and how the community needs to be more diligent and vigilant in honouring their cultures, histories and stories.

> *Alex and Eve* is an Australian movie that tells the story of two people from different cultural backgrounds who start a relationship. Alex is a quiet, unassuming school teacher whose students suspect he is gay because he doesn't have a girlfriend. His friend Paul is dating legal receptionist Claire, whose friend Eve is a lawyer.
>
> Paul and Claire plan to have Alex and Eve meet, and from the start it is an uneven and quirky relationship. But they soon fall in love — and this is where it gets complicated. Alex is Greek Orthodox and Eve is Lebanese Muslim. Both sets of parents are vehemently opposed to this relationship when they learn what is going on. To make the situation more complex, Eve's family have arranged for her to marry a Muslim man from Lebanon, Mohammed. Paul is upset and, after another disagreement with his prejudiced father, moves out of his home. Eve's brother, who at first opposed the relationship, now sees that Eve loves Alex.
>
> On the day Eve is due to wed Mohammed her brother approaches Alex and asks if he loves Eve. Discovering that Alex does in fact love Eve, he tells Alex to go after her. Alex bundles his family into his car and confronts Eve at the wedding. After initially saying that she can't be with him, she changes her mind as Alex is walking away. The two run hand in hand to the waiting bridal car, where they kiss as they are driven away from the abandoned wedding.

In *Alex and Eve* cultural differences are conquered by love. Relationships outweighed the cultural norms accepted by society in this instance. Knowing that schools may have many different cultures represented within their student body, how schools celebrate the cultural diversity needs to be carefully managed. All recognition of cultural diversity needs to be done accurately and sensitively so that people and their cultures are treated with the respect that everyone deserves. When schools have many cultures represented within them, how cultures should be celebrated needs to be considered. Adding to the equation that schools are likely to be teaching one language other than English as part of the curriculum, honouring all cultures may be a challenge. Schools need to be diligent in their efforts. An attitude of "It's all too hard" is not good enough.

Aboriginal and Torres Strait Islander peoples

The First Nations People of Australia, the Aboriginal and Torres Strait Islander people, have very distinct protocols for introductions and behaviour at public and private events. The correct use of language, behaviour and appropriate introductions are all of great importance when acknowledging Aboriginal and Torres Strait Islander cultures, histories and languages.

Some organisations have been very astute and respectful in developing protocols which they encourage people to use when honouring the traditional custodians of the land. For example, the Narragunnawali: Reconciliation in Education program developed protocols in an effort to promote the consistent use of behaviours and terminology related to the First Nations People of Australia. These protocols highlight the balance between protocols and developing and promoting positive relationships. This is an occasion where the correct use of protocols builds the relationship.

We live in a culture where enormous damage has been done to the First Nations People through lack of protocols and lack of understanding. Historically white Australians treated the Aboriginal and Torres Strait Islander peoples badly, sometimes out of ignorance, sometimes with the belief of good intentions and sometimes out of malice.

The movie *Rabbit Proof Fence* sheds light on the plight of the stolen generations. It tells the story of three young Aboriginal girls who were taken from their family and put into a boarding school. The children escaped and tried to follow the fence-line back to their family. This example of a stolen generations story typifies the actions based in the misplaced belief of acting in the best interests of Aboriginal and Torres Strait Islander peoples. It took some brave people to act outside the accepted protocols, policies, procedures, processes and practices to improve cross-cultural relationships.

In the fictional movie *Australia*, an English aristocrat and a Caucasian drover treated the Aboriginal and Torres Strait Islander peoples with respect, which was in contrast to many of the English settlers. These two characters broke the accepted protocols to build relationships with the First Nations peoples for the mutual benefit of all involved.

Using the correct protocols is a step towards reconciling the damages of the past. This is a wonderful example of how using the correct protocols will build relationships. There is still the opportunity for some degree of latitude and autonomy when working within the protocols.

For many, many years Aboriginal and Torres Strait Islander Peoples did not have the same rights as white Australians. The apology by the Prime Minister of Australia on 13 February 2008 went some way to healing the failures and wrongdoings of white Australians. As a new sign of respect for the Aboriginal and Torres Strait Islander peoples, governments and institutions began to introduce protocols, policies, procedures, processes and practices to acknowledge their histories, languages and cultures.

It is common for schools to acknowledge Country at whole-school events such as assemblies or even religious gatherings in faith-based schools. If schools have Aboriginal and Torres Strait Islander staff, they may be asked to lead the Acknowledgement of Country or Welcome to Country. When schools sing the national anthem, they should have three flags visible: the Australian flag, the Aboriginal flag and the Torres Strait Islander Flag. These flags are often provided by local politicians: local, state or federal members of parliament who are very aware of the importance of celebrating First Nations People. Schools without any Indigenous staff or students can still acknowledge Country and have the three flags on display. It is important that students are taught the correct ways for the flags to be displayed. This must be taught rather than presumed that the students know it.

Schools are also required to teach Aboriginal and Torres Strait Islander Histories and Cultures as part of the curriculum, along with Asian and Australia's Engagement with Asia, and Sustainability perspectives (ACARA 2020). This means that when teachers are teaching content they can bring in the ways that Aboriginal and Torres Strait Islander cultures may teach the same content. This can apply to most subjects, including the teaching of religious education, as First Nations People have a rich spirituality.

Celebrating Cultural Diversity

Celebrating other cultures presents a wonderful opportunity to recognise the rich tapestry of cultural diversity within schools. Multicultural awareness days allow students to celebrate their country of origin. This may mean asking their parents to share their cultural heritage, which can bring up great stories and memories for families. Schools and families may also need to be sensitive when families share stories that may trigger traumatic feelings depending on the family history. Families who have come to Australia as refugees may choose not to share much of their story, and this needs to be respected. Other families may choose to share their story as a way to build cultural awareness.

A cultural awareness day may include students wearing traditional dress, sharing food from their culture and sharing stories and traditions. This helps students celebrate their identity and can be quite a joyous occasion, where inclusion and respect can be highlighted. It also provides the opportunity for schools to celebrate how Australia has changed from its origins of Aboriginal and Torres Strait Islander custodianship to the arrival of Europeans and the historical events that saw the influx of people from the United Kingdom, Asian countries, African countries, European countries, South American countries and many others.

Schools should gather resources for teachers to use when organising such celebrations. There is rich literature available for teachers to share with the students. Teacher librarians and curriculum leaders play important roles in the support of teachers. Staff may also choose to share their own cultural background as they may be familiar with their own unique customs used to celebrate their origins. Staff may have traditional dress and may like to share traditional food.

Other ways that schools can bring cultural awareness is to use the language of another culture to greet and begin school gatherings, to sing *Happy Birthday* at school assemblies in another language, often the language taught at the school. Staff may like to greet students in their native tongue if they can learn it. My experience suggests that students appreciate the effort staff go to in learning their native tongue. A greeting in language is a simple and unique practice that can build positive relationships quickly. Coupled with the spoken word, people may choose to follow cultural norms when greeting people of culturally diverse backgrounds. Some traditions have particular rituals, such as bowing respectfully, using or avoiding eye contact, handshakes, exchanging business cards, exchanging gifts, standing directly opposite or to the side of someone or using open handed gestures when directing guests as opposed to pointing. While knowing and practising these rituals can build relationships, the reality of knowing the customs of many different traditions may prove unlikely for school communities. If there is a majority culture prevalent in a school, then those cultural norms may be learnt so a significant portion of the school may participate in these rituals.

Some cultures have strict protocols regarding gender roles. While some of these customs may be contrary to Australian customs, they should be respected, which will build the relationship, cultural awareness, inclusion and tolerance. For example, in some cultures the male partner will be the dominant communicator, leaving the female partner to be less communicative, even when engaging with school. There may be other instances where the father of a child rarely engages with school, leaving the educational responsibilities to the mother. These models work fine until a child has an issue that requires the school staff and parents to work together. Such collaboration may require teachers and ideally both parents to be involved. Introducing a silent parent to the conversation after a period of absence may prove challenging. This is another opportunity where cultural protocols may be followed to build relationships. It may also be an opportunity to gently educate the parents about cultural expectations relevant to the country where the school is based.

Dress codes may also have relevance for different cultures. While staff may not be asked to wear traditional dress, they should respect parents who choose to wear them, especially when they are visiting the school. Staff may also need to be conscious of their own dress codes, which should be respectful of the cultures with whom they are working. Dress codes can demonstrate cultural awareness as well as high professional standards. Such a simple gesture can build positive relationships.

Scenarios to Consider

Scenario 1

Context: When a school gathers for weekly assemblies, singing the Australian national anthem is considered a sign of respect for our country. A group of students who find the national anthem exclusive refuses to sing the anthem as they don't believe it represents their culture.

Dilemma: Should a teacher or principal insist and attempt to force students to sing the national anthem of Australia, especially when the students believe the anthem doesn't recognise their country of origin? Should a student be forced to sing the anthem?

Options: The school leaders may choose to explain the limitations of the wording of the anthem and the change in the Australian cultural make-up since the anthem was introduced. They may also remind the school community of the recent change of one word in the anthem ("We are one and free" has been changed from "We are young and free", suggesting that our society is united as one and recognises that Aboriginal and Torres Strait Islander heritage is not young, as it has existed for tens of thousands of years).

There is also an opportunity for the school leaders to acknowledge that the while the anthem may not be perfect, it is accepted as our national song. Realistically no-one can be forced to open their mouth and sing. Teachers may also like to invite students from other cultures to teach the school their anthems or other traditional songs and sing them on multicultural awareness days.

Scenario 2

Context: A parent from an African background has an argument on a weekend with a parent from the same country. The argument becomes a physical confrontation, with one parent seriously injured through the violence. In Africa it may be acceptable to resolve such a disagreement with physical violence. In Australia violence is illegal and considered a bad example to the younger generation. The school principal has an obligation to ensure the safety of the students, and if the two fathers were involved in a physical altercation, the safety of the students could be jeopardised.

Dilemma: Should the school principal intervene, in any capacity, to ensure the children of each family are safe when the altercation happened outside of school hours? Does the principal have a responsibility to educate the parents in culturally acceptable behaviours when resolving disagreements?

Options: The principal and teachers should check in with the children of all the families involved in the altercation. If there are cultural liaison officers available to work with the families, then the parents involved may listen to and understand advice as to what is acceptable and legal behaviour from someone with a similar cultural background. Cultural liaison officers and/or guidance counsellors need to ensure the children are safe at home.

If the relationship between the school staff and the parents is one of respect, the parents may appreciate guidance from a trusted source.

Parents from some cultures may be more comfortable communicating with a male school leader, "man to man". While this attitude is broadly considered sexist in Australian society, the reality is that men from some cultures are reluctant to listen to women with respect. If the school leader is not a man, then the parent will have to listen to the female school leader. This is a tricky scenario with no formula for guaranteed success.

Scenario 3

Context: Students of a cultural minority background within a school are being teased by other students for appearing different from the majority of students. As these students are in primary school, it is highly probable that they have been influenced by factors beyond their own experiences. These factors could be their parents or older siblings, who may have modelled prejudice, or the media.

Dilemma: Should school staff inform the parents of the racist comments by the young children? Should the principal ask questions as to where the children may have learnt such comments, especially when the school teaches inclusion and tolerance? This is a risk as parents may take offence at any suggestion that they are responsible for their child's attitude. Should school staff just work with the students and educate, and possibly punish, the children who made the racist comments as a way to promote appropriate behaviour?

Options: School leaders must educate the students demonstrating racist behaviour as to the school expectations of welcoming cultural diversity in the school community. Staff may use examples of what is appropriate language to demonstrate inclusion of different cultures. These examples may be shared with the parents of the children who made the inappropriate comments.

The victim and their parents will also require support. Unfortunately, there are ignorant and prejudiced people in the world, and while schools can educate students and families within their limits, victims of racist behaviour may need assistance to manage their response as best they can. Providing support in developing appropriate responses to inappropriate behaviours may help build resilience.

Summary

Schools benefit from embracing the cultural diversity within their communities. In celebrating diversity and promoting greater cultural awareness, schools should follow the relevant five P's and build relationships across all cultural groups. This may prove challenging where cultural groups have years of historical animosity. But recognising, embracing and practising different cultural traditions goes a long way to building tolerance, acceptance and inclusion within school communities that are rich with diversity.

"A teacher fostering a healthy classroom commits him/herself to a culture of relationships."

Michael Grinder, author

Think of your own CULTURAL DIVERSITY scenario and do a response analysis

Scenario:

Dilemma:

Options:

Response checklist:
- ☑ **Does the response improve the learning and wellbeing of students, staff and families?**
- ☑ **Workplace health and safety**: Will the action keep people safe?
- ☑ **Transparency**: Do stakeholders understand the rationale for the action?
- ☑ **Best interests of the majority**: Is the action in the best interests of the majority of stakeholders?
- ☑ **Fairness**: Does the action meet the needs of stakeholders?
- ☑ **Practicality and sustainability**: Can the action be done and continue to be done?
- ☑ **Cost-benefit analysis**: Does the cost of the action warrant the outcome?
- ☑ **Legal requirements**: Does the action meet the obligations of relevant legislation?

Chapter 10
MANAGING THROUGH UNCERTAINTY

School life presents numerous challenges for leaders as they manage teaching and learning for all students and staff along with the various other responsibilities that come with being the leader of a school. Many of the elements are part of the day-to-day life of running a school and are quite predictable. There are also days when leaders feel like they have a plan yet at the end of the day, none of their planned work was done because schools can be unpredictable. Things just happen in schools that leaders cannot predict, yet they have to respond and lead. This keeps the school dynamic challenging and rewarding for leaders. Conversely, the unpredictability can also cause stress and tension as plans may need to be flexible and evolve as uncertainty happens. Events that are unpredictable and for which school leaders may not be trained or qualified include managing a critical incident or responding to an agitated parent or staff member.

In the movie *Sergio* we are reminded of the capacity for people to break protocols to build positive relationships in tense situations. Sergio DeMello was a United Nations diplomat working around the world. The movie concentrates specifically on his mission working in Iraq soon after 9/11.

When DeMello arrived in Iraq there were numerous protocols that staff were following based on keeping everyone safe. DeMello believed that it was critical to build relationships with the locals so that they would trust the UN staff and hopefully build a better world for them. He was working on the welfare of the community outweighing the strict protocols that the UN (and the influential United States) had in place.

The movie recounts his personal life, his marriage, his relationship with his children and his new relationship with a co-worker. His professional life is retold to highlight how he managed to work in countries around the world, but most specifically Iraq, where and when there were no real precedents to follow or from which to learn. DeMello had tremendous experience on which to base his decisions, along with his desire to build relationships in support of the people with whom he was working.

Sergio describes the great uncertainty DeMello encountered in war torn countries when tasked with negotiating peace and empowering the local people. Most of what he was facing was unknown, even though he had vast experience. He could draw on this experience for what he predicted could happen, while being flexible and responsive to the unknown of each new mission. It was uncertainty that provided the greatest challenge.

School leaders understand and accept the unpredictable nature of their work. When major events happen school leaders face the challenge of navigating unchartered waters for which there may be no guidebook to follow. For example, natural disasters such as floods, fires and earthquakes may cause schools to close. This may result in students having to work from home, with teachers responsible for providing work if and when possible. In recent times the world was shut down as the COVID-19 coronavirus impacted the lifestyle of people around the world.

During the management of the global COVID-19 pandemic politicians and community leaders faced great uncertainty. They were charged with making decisions in the best interests of the public in order to keep members of the public safe from the virus. The leaders were responding to new situations which provided unprecedented challenges. The task was not easy, and the decisions made were not always understood or popular. Community leaders were making decisions which also included the response to education during this time. How education was delivered during the pandemic was new for many people. These were times of great uncertainty and education was affected along with many professions.

In schools leaders have been asked to manage changing circumstances very quickly in accommodating alternative education provision, otherwise known as home-schooling, along with changing restrictions regarding physical distancing, parents' access to school and the wearing of masks. This chapter unpacks why it is critical to have the five P's in place while building relationships in times of uncertainty.

The global pandemic has seen people justify behaviours through the welfare and safety of everybody. School leaders had to manage the needs of the students, staff and families while still providing high-quality teaching and learning. There were protocols to follow while caring about the relationships with the school community. This uncertainty posed questions for leaders. Did following the protocols outweigh building relationships with people who were becoming highly stressed and agitated? Were there exceptional reasons why those five P's could be breached or broken in favour of building relationships in a time that was exceedingly stressful for everybody? This was a balancing act for which no-one was trained.

Alternative Education Provision

The pandemic has seen families, teachers and students working in unprecedented times, particularly with the need for alternative education provision – colloquially known as home-schooling, remote learning or alternative education provision depending on the jurisdiction. It is now more important than ever that teachers and parents trust each other, collaborate together and ask relevant questions to ensure that children's learning can still continue. There are a few topics which may assist in guiding parents and teachers to work together whenever they are delivering education in a unique way. The use of language is critical when managing times of perceived crisis. If we use the global pandemic as an example of managing through uncertainty, the lessons learned can be applied to other crises.

There have been countless media reports, various correspondence and communications that come out from government, health and education authorities. These frequently use emotive language when they talk about the crisis and the stress that affects us all in these new times. If there is minimal use of emotive language, there may be less stress on the lives of families, staff and students as they navigate through these uncharted waters. But it is still important to understand the magnitude of the situation in which we are living.

COVID-19 is very serious and it needs to be managed carefully. Behaviours and habits that we need to practice and enforce to keep everyone safe and healthy are critical. However, for students the message needs to emphasise that this is a new way of doing things. While teachers are identifying ways to provide education and learning experiences, it does not necessarily need to be stressful, though it will certainly be new. The language that parents, teachers and education and medical authorities use needs to be realistic, yet it doesn't always need to be emotive and worrying for the general population. Here is the first part to balance: be honest with the communication while being conscious of the impact on the emotional toll of the people.

When teachers are communicating with parents and with students we need to talk about new experiences and we need to talk about unprecedented times. Educators need to talk about uncharted waters. We don't need to use words such as "stressful time" or "worrying times"; we just need to talk about "new experiences" or a "new ways of doing things". The reality is that there are going to be some positive outcomes as a result of these experiences. Society may end up with more highly skilled teachers in delivering curriculum in alternate ways. Communities may end up with new ways of communicating effectively. Education authorities may also end up with schools that have had the opportunity to attend to matters that always get put on the backburner due to the business of our jobs. Everyone can take the opportunity to look on the positive side of what are challenging new times.

Parents may have been at home with their children for a period of time while home-schooling has been necessary, where they needed to support their child's learning. Parents may have been playing a far more active role than they do when their child is at school for five or six hours a day. Teachers are often called upon to offer advice for parents as to how best to structure the learning opportunities for their children.

Teacher Advice for Parents

Seeking advice is one of the five reasons why parents engage with the staff of their children's school. During the uncertainty of children being home-schooled during the pandemic, parents were seeking advice about how best to make home-schooling work. While home-schooling was new for the majority of educators and families, sharing of ideas about how to make it productive has been available (Sweatman and Oberthur 2020; see Appendix B).

Establishing a routine and a timetable for children and families is a good place to start for home-schooling. This means that children will know what to expect when they get up in the morning. They will go through the usual daily routines of having breakfast and getting dressed and making their bed, and then they can expect that they are going to be engaging with some learning. This routine will provide some basic protocols for learning while at home. Now more than ever relationships are important. Parents were faced with balancing keeping positive relationships while making an effort to follow the school's recommended model for learning at home.

Most children value and appreciate knowing the direction of each day. If children have a timetable that can be displayed, be it through pictures or through words, and it's put in a central place or in a learning space that parents and the children have created, then they can work towards tracking and monitoring what needs to be done. Once something is completed, once the first activity is done, tick it off. It gives the child and the supervising parents a sense of achievement. So first let's have a timetable. Let's have a dedicated learning space, if in fact there is an area in the home that that can be set up. I think it's also important that parents understand that when children are at school they are engaged for somewhere between five and six hours of learning each day. This will not be the same at home. Let's be a realistic and aim for children to engage in learning between maybe two to three hours depending on the age of the child. Certainly high school children have the capacity to work significantly longer than children in primary school. Children in primary school between the ages of five and 12 can engage with learning activities for between two to three hours over the course of a day. Parents should be very proud of their own achievements and be very proud of their children's achievements. With home-schooling much relies on parents supervising their children's engagement, even though the teachers will still be providing the curriculum through various platforms. This is a very structured model that may not work for all families. It may in fact be new to families who have to work within a model that suits their family. The parents will have to balance managing the children's work commitments with harmonious relationships at home.

Speaking of platforms, it is important that parents and carers understand the platforms that teachers may be using to deliver curriculum and to provide feedback. Some schools may have their own e-learning platforms. Other schools will use platforms such as MS Teams, SeeSaw, OneDrive or OneNote. Whatever the product, parents must be knowledgeable of the relevant platforms their children will be using during any period of home-schooling. That's the process necessary to build relationships remotely to remain connected.

It will be important for parents, and children, to have breaks during the day, both physical breaks (get up, walk around, stretch their legs, go outside) as well as a mental breaks (switch off from the activity that the children have been doing). Once the activities are completed, parents need to provide some feedback for the student or be able to send it back to the teachers via technology. Parents shouldn't feel obliged to give feedback instantaneously. They should have mental and physical breaks regularly throughout the day. Home-schooling is a whole new world, and parents and students and teachers need to be kind to each other so that together we can continue the child's learning while looking after our mental and physical wellbeing. Connection and relationships are important! These relationships need to exist while working within some protocols necessary for learning to continue.

When people have to physically isolate when required, it is important that students, teachers and families maintain social contacts as best they can with the use of technology. Parents need to ensure they can allow their children access to their friends via technology, be it via video conferencing and the various platforms that are available to families or via telephone. Similarly, parents also need to maintain regular contact with their own parent networks. Whether or not school parents and friends still maintain contact, parents have their own social networks and it will be important for the parents mental and social wellbeing to still keep in touch with other parents, because whatever is happening at home for them and their children, something similarly may be happening to children and other parents in other families around their communities. Respecting the safety protocols should ensure people remain safe.

There are numerous learning opportunities available at home that parents may have not considered as valuable learning opportunities. These opportunities may be above and beyond the curriculum that the teachers are delivering. Literacy learning must continue every day, as it ordinarily does. Children should be reading every day. It doesn't really matter what the reading is as long as the material is age-appropriate. It could be the newspaper, it could be a comic, it could be a recipe book, it could be a magazine, it could be a novel or it could be an encyclopaedia or other non-fiction material. Whatever the children enjoy reading, parents must encourage them to read and then teachers can encourage them to respond to that reading through writing or, if age-appropriate, through drawing.

Give children the opportunity first to be reading every day and then to do some form of writing. They may in fact like to keep a diary. As long as children are reading every day and they can have a written response to their reading their literacy will continue to develop. Parents can always listen to them read aloud. They can also give them feedback about their writing, including spelling and grammar. It is very important that children maintain their English literacy throughout any period of home-schooling. Ideally parents can support the school's practices in guiding the children's reading habits.

Some other basic household activities which provide fantastic learning opportunities for students at home will include activities like cooking. The amount of maths that is involved in cooking is tremendous. Children will be able to engage with measurement, counting, estimating and geometry – all important mathematical skills that cooking incidentally provides. While it might be a challenge for parents to think they are going to have their child helping them in the kitchen to cook, parents are encouraged to embrace the learning opportunities that can go with cooking. It may also encourage children to have a healthy lifestyle. (It may also give them an appreciation of what parents have to do in preparing meals).

When children want to get outside, encourage them to explore the garden and around the house, where there are numerous opportunities to encourage some of their science learning. Children may go into the garden and track the growth of a plant. They can go and explore the insects that are in and around the garden. There are various opportunities that nature can provide which will enhance children's learning. Parents should make sure children have mental breaks and when they do get them outside engage with nature. If they're asking questions, that's fantastic. If parents don't know the answer, that allows them to go and explore further and search for answers.

While parents may be somewhat fearful or cautious about the amount of time their child may be spending online the during a time of home-schooling, the reality is that they will need to limit the child's amount of screen time, as they should do every week. There is no doubt that being on screens will provide some opportunities for learning. Let's not deny the reality that our families face in having technology available to their children. Teachers will be delivering the curriculum and other messages via online platforms. There are significant learning opportunities available online for children, so parents may need to embrace that opportunity. Parents can still limit the amount of screen time while reminding children they can have some fun on screens.

During this new time and unprecedented time teachers, parents and students need to trust each other more than ever. They need to collaborate more than ever. They need to be asking the right questions more than ever so that we can continue to provide learning opportunities for all children. Parents need to monitor their own levels of calmness, and if those levels deteriorate, parents are encouraged to share the workload around. If children have two parents at home, the parents will need to share the responsibility. If children only have one parent at home, single parents may need to network with others so that they have a break for themselves. During this time parents still remain parents. While they are adopting the role of pseudo teacher, they are still the child's parents and the teachers will still be providing the curriculum, even though it will be through a new mode of delivery. So parents remain as parents, teachers remain as teachers, and both should work together collaboratively. If there are any issues, parents and teachers are encouraged to ask the right and relevant questions. We must continue to trust and collaborate so that we can still provide a high-quality learning for the students.

Home-schooling emphasises the importance of connecting and maintaining relationships. The protocols and processes may be articulated to the families, yet the ability for the teachers to influence or enforce the protocols are minimal. History indicates that periods of home-schooling do not harm the students' overall academic performance. And anecdotally, home-schooling gives parents a greater appreciation for teachers. While teachers have greater understanding of the demands of parents juggling multiple roles at home as parent, "teacher", counsellor and play supervisor. Home-schooling can't rely on processes, procedures, practices, protocols or policies, only guidelines which can direct the parents. Relationships need to be maintained and strengthened if possible.

School Issues

Now let's consider some challenging issues where leaders have to balance protocols and relationships under the unusual conditions of the global pandemic. How do schools manage the process of providing high-quality home-schooling when students may have varied access to the necessary technology to ensure an equitable, fair and just education provision to all students? Following are some of the dilemmas that leaders have had to resolve while balancing building relationships within strict and often unprecedented protocols. Again, these issues can be applied to other crises where students may have to learn from home.

Dispositions for Learning at Home and School

During home schooling, traditional school protocols are put in hibernation while teachers and families work together to provide an education for their children. I use the possessive pronoun "their", as both parents and teachers have responsibility for the education of children. According to Jill Sweatman, The Brain Whisperer™, the conditions necessary for students to learn are safety, connectedness and contentment (see Appendix A). As a result of recent events, which saw most children learning at home under the guidance of their parents and the direction of their teachers and now having returned to school, these three conditions necessary for a child to learn are relevant in any setting. The conditions, or personal dispositions, are universally applicable to children everywhere.

The first of these dispositions is **safety**.

First and foremost, for a child to be in a position to learn they must feel safe. Their safety means they have enough food, clothing and shelter, the basics for living a healthy life, so they can then concentrate on the task of learning. Food, clothing and shelter would ordinarily be provided by their parents or carers. However, in some circumstances, it is necessary for the school to take on that responsibility of providing food on occasions for a child. Breakfast clubs are quite common across schools in Australia, whereby children who come from family environments that don't have the capacity to provide breakfast for children rely on the school to provide food, so the child has enough sustenance to concentrate in class. Clothing is occasionally also provided by schools. Second-hand or even brand new uniforms may be provided for children who cannot be provided with adequate uniforms by their families. Uniforms help children feel like they belong as they look the same as their classmates. The family home is the shelter in which most children live. Occasionally children may be living with other caring adults. As long as they "have a roof over their heads" the third essential basic requirement is provided. Other caring adults may include grandparents, other relatives, foster carers and family friends. Sleeping in a warm bed is important for children. The other element about being safe is that children know and understand their routines in life. They know who will be dropping them at school. They know who will be picking them up at school. They have the confidence to walk out of the school gate at the end of the day knowing that someone who knows and loves them will be there waiting for them. These are all elements of a child feeling safe so that they can attend to the task of learning at school.

The second disposition is **connectedness**.

A child needs to be connected with their family and their social networks beyond their family. These networks can include their school or any cultural activities such as sport or artistic pursuits. Connection begins before birth, in the womb, then through their toddler years, through to when they join a school group. Initially the child should be connected with their family, their parents and their grandparents who know and love them. Then when a child moves to school they will ideally find children of similar interests, potentially like-minded children with whom they will make a connection and form part of a group. The connections between a child and their parents and a child and their school groups are critical to the child being part of a social group which knows and cares about them. Being part of a group is key to a child's wellbeing because human beings are social beings. We know, live, love, learn and work together. It is very rare that human beings function in isolation and hence being connected to a social group, their family and their friends, is very important for a child's wellbeing and welfare.

The third disposition that is essential for a child to be able to learn is **contentment**.

Originally I thought the third disposition might have been happiness, but my wise colleague Jill Sweatman reminded us that happiness is an elevated state of joy that not everyone will reach, but everyone can reach contentment. My definition of contentment is that there is a degree of acceptance of someone's current circumstances or lifestyle. A child needs to accept their place in life. They need to accept the family in which they live, they need to accept the school which they attend, they need to accept the social group of which they are a part, they need to accept the limitations of their personal circumstances and they need to accept (and embrace) the opportunities that life presents them. If a child is accepting, they have a degree of contentment, tolerance and understanding of their disposition in life. This then allows them to focus on the task at hand at school, which is learning. Children who are content and have an acceptance and an understanding of their circumstances may even find opportunities to embrace beyond their family and school life. They already have a degree of solitude and comfort in themselves and their social network. Knowing that they are safe and knowing that they are connected allows them to explore other opportunities beyond those two dispositions. Please note that acceptance of the limitations of their current circumstances does not mean that people should not strive to go beyond those situations for improvement. Striving to improve and excel should be a goal for all lifelong learners.

All three dispositions are inextricably linked. It is not possible to be connected without being safe. It is not possible to be content without being connected. And it is not possible to be safe without being a connected. All three dispositions are essential for a child to be able to attend to learning at school and beyond school.

In 2022 there was a major flood which effected south-east Queensland and northern New South Wales. This meant schools were closed for a brief period of time. In 2020 and 2021 children from across the country, and across the globe, have had periods of learning at home due to COVID-19. Using this experience, we can apply some lessons of managing through uncertainty to other crises.

When children are learning from home there is a degree of physical isolation from their social groups. However, technology has ensured children can still feel connected through the use of various platforms, which allow face-to-face connections through the virtual world. Physical isolation has also been a test of resilience for children, their families and school staff. Teachers were also missing the presence of seeing the children's smiling faces in front of them. Thankfully technology has at least allowed some connection through the medium of online platforms. Similarly, through the experience of educating during COVID-19, the families, children and staff that accepted the positions they were placed in and the limitations within which they had to operate have probably adjusted more quickly and hence may have been more successful and less stressed in understanding and accepting the current circumstances in which they were working.

It was critical that teachers and parents were on the same page about the priorities that needed to be addressed when they were operating in educational isolation. It was critical that teachers and parents understood that a child had to be safe first and foremost. The child had to know that they were loved; that they had food, clothing and shelter; and that their teacher would be providing work for them. It was important that teachers and parents maintained a degree of social connection for the child, and the child should have been able to connect with their classmates and their teachers through technology. It was also critical that parents, teachers and students accepted the limitations in which they were working. Learning from home during COVID-19 was most unusual. The delivery of curriculum, the ability to provide feedback, the ability give one-on-one instruction and the ability to give group instruction was different than what it would be if a teacher was standing in front of the class. Teachers did a fantastic job in adapting their delivery, feedback and support of the children during this time. They had to have a degree of acceptance and contentment about the circumstances in which they were working.

If a child is safe, connected and content, they have the opportunity to switch on and to attend to the task at hand at school. Having returned to school recently, it has been evident that the children who weren't safe, who may not have been connected and who were struggling with the changing circumstances over the last few months may have struggled to attend to learning. We can reinforce these dispositions of safety, connection and contentment so that children will learn (Sweatman and Oberthur 2020). Once a child has these dispositions, they have the capacity to be receptive to learning. If any one of these three dispositions is missing, threatened or jeopardised, the child's capacity to learn is significantly impeded.

Scenarios to Consider

Scenario 1

Context: Every family responds differently to the demands of home-schooling. When schools were thrown into immediate lockdowns school leaders were asked to manage the provision of alternate education models for their students while ensuring the staff were well positioned to provide home-schooling. Not all parents could provide the leadership at home for their children. Not all families had access to the technology required for their children to access the curriculum provided by the teachers, and some parents would not allow their children to use home devices.

Dilemma: Should schools provide devices for families who say they don't have access to sufficient devices? And if parents will not allow their children to use home devices, should the school provide reading books for these students? If so, how should the school manage the process of distribution and collection?

Options: Schools may use available technology resources to provide students with devices if required. They may choose to identify which grades are in most need of devices (usually upper primary school and high school students). This means students in the younger grades may be provided with activities that don't require devices.

Schools may develop processes for the distribution and collection of resources, including reading books, if they can do so within the health guidelines. Schools may also advise parents of ways to access resources without visiting schools; for example, using reading books from local libraries or even books from home. Reading material can also be found online. Teachers need to stand in the shoes of the parents to accommodate their needs.

Scenario 2

Context: Each teacher responds differently to the demands placed on them by new models of delivery. Some teachers may enjoy the challenge, while others may get stressed and anxious about the impact of such a change. Some teachers when thrown the curveball of teaching online found the demands very challenging. Delivering the curriculum via a computer has required teachers to improve their computer skills, become familiar with presenting online and manage remote communication with colleagues and parents.

Dilemma: Should a principal expect the same level of delivery from all teachers, knowing their computer skill levels vary? Should principals provide additional support for teachers who are slower to adapt than their colleagues?

Options: School leaders need be explicit and transparent about their expectations of staff when delivering the curriculum. School leaders need to set the expectations for all teachers about a variety of topics for the teachers so there is consistency in the delivery and management of home-schooling. Teachers will appreciate knowing the school leader's expectations regarding frequency of communication with students and parents, how planning and delivery of the curriculum will be managed and how and when feedback will be provided to students. School leaders also need to arrange how and when they will monitor their staff's wellbeing through regular check-ins.

Scenario 3

Context: Teachers have very little influence over what happens at home for families who are managing home-schooling. Families with multiple children mean additional demands on parents who have to provide guidance, possibly simultaneously, to their students during home-schooling. Some parents may choose to abandon following the home-schooling model as recommended by the school. This presents a moral and ethical challenge for the school staff, especially when the students return to school.

Dilemma: When parents "switch off" and choose to abandon the home-schooling model as prescribed by the teachers, should principals engage with the parents and ask them for more support at home? When the students return to school and there is a variety of the amount work returned, should teachers provide feedback to individuals or should they start teaching from where they left their teaching before home-schooling? Should teachers focus on the basics of English and maths or continue covering the full curriculum and play "catch up" with the subjects they didn't address during home-schooling?

Options: Teachers need to work with their colleagues to determine how best to respond to students so there is consistency within year levels and across the grades at school. For families who have disengaged during home-schooling, teachers need to be compassionate towards the students and do their best to support the students' learning. Teachers will need to identify a common recommencement point from which to resume teaching face-to-face.

There will be expectations from education authorities as to how to play "catch up" when students return. Schools will develop a plan for students so teachers can teach under the new circumstances as necessary.

Summary

One of the necessary traits of a good teacher and good school leaders is the ability to adapt quickly, especially in times of uncertainty. This has been tested and stretched since the global pandemic forced schools to provide alternative education models for home-schooling on short notice. While the delivery of the curriculum remains the core business of schools, keeping students, families and staff connected during uncertain times has also been a priority. Keeping everyone safe, connected and content allows for high-quality teaching and learning.

During these times of uncertainty school leaders have developed new protocols to allow them to provide high-quality teaching and learning while providing a compassionate response to the needs of their staff, students and families. School leaders need to balance what is important in times of uncertainty, building relationships within the protocols.

"While bad leaders make stressful situations worse, good leaders bring out the best in us."

Simon Sinek, optimist and author

Think of your own MANAGING THROUGH UNCERTAINTY scenario and do a response analysis

Scenario:

Dilemma:

Options:

Response checklist:
- ☑ **Does the response improve the learning and wellbeing of students, staff and families?**
- ☑ **Workplace health and safety**: Will the action keep people safe?
- ☑ **Transparency**: Do stakeholders understand the rationale for the action?
- ☑ **Best interests of the majority**: Is the action in the best interests of the majority of stakeholders?
- ☑ **Fairness**: Does the action meet the needs of stakeholders?
- ☑ **Practicality and sustainability**: Can the action be done and continue to be done?
- ☑ **Cost-benefit analysis**: Does the cost of the action warrant the outcome?
- ☑ **Legal requirements**: Does the action meet the obligations of relevant legislation?

CONCLUSION

On 8 January 2021 Australia's Prime Minister, Scott Morrison, said in response to the new measures to be taken to manage the UK strain of coronavirus, "We certainly don't want the protections to be worse than the impact". This begs the question as to what measures the government could put in place to ensure that relationships are maintained and protocols are followed without jeopardising the welfare and relationships in our communities. Since the global pandemic has impacted on the lives of Australians and millions around the world, leaders have had to balance keeping their constituents safe, keeping businesses viable, keeping the economy moving, looking after the welfare of the people and being consistent in their implementation of rules that were created as the world changed, sometimes overnight. Juggling those various criteria is a complex task and there is no one-size-fits-all model to guide leaders.

Jill Sweatman said to me once, "It takes a strong leader to maintain protocols at risk of public opinion". Imagine then the strength it takes to be a political leader in times of national or global change. Or imagine being a school leader who has to juggle many policies, protocols, procedures and practices while providing a high-quality education for all students. These are two examples of leaders with a significant number of "clients" (constituents and families/students), although on different scales, who need to promote the welfare of their people while having to make decisions, sometimes unpopular decisions, in the best interests of the majority of people.

Making decisions that are based on matters of life and death are challenging. When rules are put in place to minimise the impact of a crisis such as a global pandemic, floods, fires or earthquakes, leaders simply justify their tough decisions to change people's access to their normal lifestyles by saying that it is a matter of life and death, or at least a matter of personal and community safety. Makes sense. Simple. Easy. Who could debate that rationale? The economic cost, the loss of business and the uncertainty of returning to "normal" are all issues that the general public have the right to ask about.

Allan Parker, a forensic linguist and behavioural scientist, once said to me, "When engaging in any human interaction, the person entering the dialogue should ask themselves some questions which [allow] them to be positive and promote positive relationships:

♦   Do I have permission to enter the dialogue?
♦   Is it in the best interests of the other parties?
♦   Is it in my best interests?"

When leaders are making decisions, ideally they do so in the best interests of all people and filter their decisions with criteria. These criteria may include things such as the safety of all people, the economic benefits for all people and the mental welfare of all people. Of course, every person responds differently in times of change and times of crisis, and hence leaders will be making decisions that they believe will benefit the most people. Needless to say, it is a huge challenge and would cause leaders some consternation when making decisions of tremendous magnitude that affect many, many people within their communities. When leaders do make controversial decisions they are often judged by their public or their people. Individuals will make a judgment based on the impact on their personal lives. They may also make an opinion based on the impact on the lives of the majority of the people. They may indeed form an opinion based on the emotional bank account that the leaders have created throughout the decisions made historically.

As long as leaders are making decisions in the best interests of the majority of people, they are also, inadvertently or intentionally, following or creating protocols, processes, procedures policies and practices which they expect and anticipate people will follow. If leaders have credit in the emotional bank account, they are in a position to negotiate harder decisions. If leaders don't have credit in the emotional bank account and make decisions without consultation and collaboration, then their people, followers, constituents or clients are less likely to be graciously accepting of their decisions. In such cases people will feel that the protocols, processes, procedures, policies and practices have been imposed without due care and thought for their wellbeing and welfare. It is therefore advisable for leaders to consult and collaborate, and this will be more successful if they already have emotional credit in the relationship bank account with their people.

It's important that relationships can be established to create harmonious relationships while keeping people safe and acting the best interests of the majority of people. So how does one build emotional credit with their people when they are just starting out? It's an important question to discuss and analyse when we're talking about building positive relationships while balancing the five P's. When a new leader starts in a position within an organisation, they need to establish relationships; they need to establish credibility; and they need to establish their leadership while working within accepted processes, protocols, procedures, policies and practices with a view to improving the community in whatever field it may be: education, politics, business or sport. They need to be astute in their decisions, collaborative in their processes and consultative in their deliberations so they can establish credit in the emotional bank account.

Leaders need to listen to their fellow leaders in an organisation before making any decisions. They need to understand the culture, context and climate of the organisation they are leading and working in before they make any decisions of significance. They need to build credit in the emotional bank account before they make any significant changes too. There will be occasions where a leader is mandated by their governing authority to make changes of significance quickly. These are often times of great stress for leaders and organisations if they are genuinely concerned about the welfare and wellbeing of the members of their community. It is a time of tension in balancing processes, policies procedures, protocols and practices while establishing relationships, if in fact that's possible where you have to make some hard decisions very quickly as a new leader in an organisation.

Simon Sinek, a British-American optimist, motivational speaker and author, talks about the importance of leaders displaying empathy and vulnerability. By leaders looking at themselves they become aware of how their professional relationships develop and are strengthened by being "human". Employees appreciate seeing the human side of leaders as it makes them more relatable. The human connections that leaders make with employees are key to building relationships and managing the protocols. Leaders who can build positive relationships with their community are well placed to balance the necessary protocols, procedures, practices, processes and policies for the good of all stakeholders in their communities. Leadership is about the three R's – relationships, relationships, relationships.

It is important for leaders to listen. It is important for leader to ask questions and to understand context and history and culture of an organisation. It is important that leaders draw on their own experience. It is important that leaders can compare and discern the value of past experiences in a new context so that they may add value to the new community and the organisation. In doing so, leaders are likely to form positive relationships with their community and hence put credit in the emotional bank account, putting them in a better position to consult, collaborate and discern wisely when making decisions that may alter the five P's.

Some of the criteria used by leaders to determine decisions in the best interests of the majority of people include concepts such as the safety of all people involved. They may include financial and economic benefits or hardships as a result of the decision for the majority of the people involved. Criteria may also include the welfare of all those people or the majority of the people involved and impact of the decision to be made. Decisions that build confidence within a community are made with a degree of care, compassion and consistency so that people know what to expect if a repeated decision needs to be made.

The inconsistencies that political leaders display during the management of crises and times of uncertainty may cause great debate and great concern. This is why people like transparency, and this is why people like consistency of protocols, processes, practices, procedures and policies. When such inconsistencies exist it causes great debate and consternation. When leaders make decisions that don't appear to show compassion and care, people start to ask questions and wonder how such a decision can be made.

So what would a reasonable person do? Would a reasonable person say we cannot deviate from the five P's for a minute risk of community harm or would a reasonable person say let's put measures in place to allow families to spend time with their loved ones? It takes a very strong leader to stand in opposition to public opinion, to stand in opposition to what most would believe a reasonable person would do and to follow procedures, practices, procedures, policies and protocols despite what probably their emotional intelligence is telling them to do.

When leaders make such decisions about maintaining policies, processes, practices, procedures and protocols, they are often very direct in their communication. This is necessary to avoid ambiguity. When leaders mitigate their message by being ambiguous, vague, gentle or subtle in their delivery it creates uncertainty and inconsistency in the response of the people. Such inconsistency erodes confidence, trust and clarity. And it's important to have confidence and clarity and trust even when decisions made may appear very harsh, unjust and uncaring. That is one of the reasons why political leaders and health officials are in a position to make such decisions and the community, while struggling with the decision, do appreciate the decision because it is clear.

People generally like consistency. People generally like routines. People generally like clear directions and instructions. There are certainly people who are free-spirited, quite happy to go with the flow and can adapt to change very quickly and very easily. The majority of people do appreciate consistency and clarity. Some people would appreciate greater consultation and collaboration. Other people are quite happy to follow and have a philosophy and a mindset of "Just tell me what to do and I'll do it". Whatever the mindset of the people with whom leaders work, and there will be many, they just have to be consistent, clear and articulate in their delivery of messages so that their people can understand and follow the decisions. Leaders cannot afford to mitigate their delivery of messages, which will create inconsistencies, ambiguities and therefore jeopardise the safety and welfare of the community. While it may appear as if leaders are trying to micromanage the behaviour of their people, it is essential that messages are not diminished or downplayed so that people are clear about the expectations leaders have provided. Now, this is stressing the importance of practices, policies, processes, procedures and protocols because there are times and places where they are critical to be implemented. It's at times when the welfare and the safety and the health of the majority of the people are being compromised that such decisions need to be made.

According to Gladwell (2008, p. 194), "We mitigate when we are being polite, or when we're ashamed or embarrassed, or when we're being deferential to authority". In the analysis of some plane crashes mitigating language was identified in the communication between the pilot and their first officers, who are less-experienced co-pilots. When the first officers were in charge of flying and the pilot was their assistant and the first officer needed correcting, the pilot gave direct and specific instructions and hence avoided accidents. "They were talking to a subordinate. They had no fear of being blunt. The first officers, on the other hand, were talking with their boss, and so they overwhelmingly chose the mitigating alternative. They hinted." (Gladwell 2008, p. 195) This had catastrophic consequences on occasions where the plane crashed, in part because the first officer couldn't be direct in their instructions to their superior.

One of the greatest challenges that leaders face when making such decisions is to act in a compassionate way that considers the mental and physical wellbeing of the people they're serving. The word "serving" is intentional here, because while leaders have to lead and make decisions they are also there at the installation or the election of the people they serve. This is certainly the case for political leaders, and it may also be the case for business leaders. It may not be the case for education leaders, who are appointed by a higher authority. It is the case, though, that leaders need to make decisions that consider the mental and physical wellbeing of the people they are serving.

Political and health leaders managing the responses to the global current pandemic may be saying they're acting in the best interest of the majority of the community. Communities couldn't afford the risk of community transmission, hence people have had to live in lockdown in certain circumstances. They have had to balance that decision of following very strict protocols, processes, procedures, protocols and practices while managing the mental and physical wellbeing of the people they are serving. They've had to manage the relationships with their people, at what could potentially be a career-changing moment, to ensure the safety of the majority of people.

Education

For school leaders, there are seemingly endless policies, practices, procedures, processes and protocols that they are required to follow. The people, communities, families and students with whom school leaders work all appreciate consistency, as do staff. Yet when people ask principals, headmasters or rectors to bend, break or deviate from the policies, practices, procedures, processes and protocols, those requesting such deviation are thinking about their best interests and are thinking about what may benefit them the most. When it comes to making decisions such as those school leaders make, if they have the capacity to deviate from the five P's, leaders have to understand that they are setting a precedent every time they make a change.

People appreciate consistency and clarity in decisions from school leaders, and that they will also act in their best interests. When a family approaches a school leader and asks, "May I deviate from the expected policies, practices, procedures, processes and protocols?", they are probably only thinking in their best interests. If the school leader says "Yes" and gives them permission to deviate from the five Ps, the leader's credibility and decision-making processes may be questioned – and that's okay. The decision school leaders have to make are generally not life-threatening. It is not something of the magnitude of flying a plane or performing surgery. It is not something of the magnitude of the coronavirus that impacts millions of people. The decision that business leaders may make may also not have the same impact.

Such a decision by school and business leaders may in fact build relationships. It may add to the emotional bank account. It may build a leader's credibility when they show flexibility to operate outside the five P's if it is in the best interest of an individual, and that's okay also. Should a leader have to explain their decisions to other members of the community? On occasions yes, and on other occasions no. Such decisions come with experience, wisdom, the support of colleagues, understanding of the culture and the context of the community. As you can see, there is no one-size-fits-all approach. And there are no easy blueprints to follow when making such decisions. I would suggest it is wise for new leaders and experienced leaders to follow the five P's relatively closely until they have built an emotional bank account with their community and until they have the experience to understand the impact of deviating from the five P's.

Sporting legend Michael Jordan is quoted as saying, "If you quit once it becomes a habit. Never quit". There is another train of thought in the book *Range* by David Epstein, which suggests that it is necessary to quit and change directions on occasions. Both trains of thought have great merit. Both trains of thought are based on years of experience and wisdom. Michael Jordan was possibly the greatest basketball player to have played the game. David Epstein's work is based on years of research and study of great leaders in various walks of life. Whether or not someone quits isn't the issue. The issue is why someone would quit and why someone would deviate from a course of action. If a leader has to make a decision that deviates from the accepted processes, policies, procedures, protocols and practices, they may be in a position to improve the welfare and wellbeing of their community. It takes a very wise leader to deviate from a course of action with a degree of confidence that will benefit the majority of people. Is quitting okay? Yes. Should people quit when things get tough? Not necessarily. It just takes a wise, experienced leader to know when to quit and to know when to pursue their course of action. It takes a wise, experienced leader with emotional intelligence to know when to build relationships and when to stand firm in following the five P's.

Brisbane Catholic Education have been proactive in upskilling their leaders by introducing a Compliance Capability Program. The program is designed to give their leaders the skills and knowledge in understanding ethical and legal responsibilities in leading schools. Leaders have obligations to act legally and ethically. Coupled with this responsibility is the moral obligation to build relationships within their communities. Does one responsibility outweigh the other? Are the two issues mutually compatible or mutually incompatible? Or can leaders balance building positive relationships within the protocols?

School leaders have enormous responsibility to ensure the safety of their employees, the provision of high-quality education for all students and a welcoming environment for families and visitors. They have to do all this within an ever-increasing list of processes, protocols, procedures, policies and practices. It is near impossible for school leaders to have intimate knowledge of all the five P's. Hence the advantage of working as part of a team, which allows the delegation of responsibilities to provide a collective wisdom.

Dr Don Parker, School Principal in Evergreen Park, Illinois shared this story on LinkedIn:

"I was really offended today at work by one of my superiors.
That's why I'm doing a late Friday night workout to burn off the stress.

District office officials joined us on walk throughs to monitor instruction.
Afterwards I was reprimanded because one of my superiors told me that
a particular teacher should be written up because she was doing a social
and emotional learning activity for 5 minutes before starting her lesson.

My superior told me that time on task and maximizing instructional
minutes were more important.

I told her that this particular teacher had recently lost her mom and 3 students in her class have also had deaths in their family this past month. She replied well she should send those kids to the social worker and focus on teaching reading and leave her baggage at the door!

I said the discussions help her and her students cope. Then I told her that telling a teacher who just suffered a crisis to leave their baggage at the door and just teach is like telling kids who suffer from adverse childhood experiences to just show up and learn!

I said we have to take care of the whole teacher just like we have to teach the whole child!

Am I wrong? Should I be telling my teachers to put the curriculum ahead of my students social and emotional health?"

Dr Parker's story illustrates perfectly how leaders need to balance building relationships with protocols, and he should be applauded for his stance.

Schools are preparing our leaders of, and for, the future. We need education to get "it" right. So if schools are hamstrung by the five P's that constrict the great work of the teachers, something needs to change.

Is our world overregulated? Are the education systems overregulated? Do the five P's build confidence among the staff, students and families? Possibly. Is there ever any conflict or stress created by the five P's? Most definitely. Is there an easy answer? No. Let's try balancing.

Allow me to repeat the premise of this book from the introduction. Here is the key question that we should keep at the forefront of our mind:

Does this improve the learning and wellbeing of students, staff and families?

Remembering that, in answering this question, we should consider the following factors:
- **Workplace health and safety**: Will the action keep people safe?
- **Transparency**: Do stakeholders understand the rationale for the action?
- **Best interests of the majority**: Is the action in the best interests of the majority of stakeholders?
- **Fairness**: Does the action meet the needs of stakeholders?

- **Practicality and sustainability**: Can the action be done and continue to be done?
- **Cost-benefit analysis**: Does the cost of the action warrant the outcome?
- **Legal requirements**: Does the action meet the obligations of relevant legislation?

> *"Being a good teacher is not about the training you have,*
> *it is not about how well you set up your classroom,*
> *the brand of materials you purchase or the amount of*
> *times your children have achieved high grades.*
>
> *Teaching is a philosophy that lives deep in your heart,*
> *in every word you say,*
> *every step you take and every time you model behaviour*
> *you wish to be reflected within the community.*
>
> *Teaching is so much more than a job,*
> *it is a belief that each and every person has the*
> *ability to change the world for the better."*

Gavin McCormack,
School Principal of the Year finalist 2020,
TEDx Speaker, 6–12 Montessori teacher

McCormack is emphasising that teaching and leading in schools is more than the process of instructing. It is about a passion for seeing students thrive. That is only possible through relationships.

Teaching and school leadership is about the three R's – relationships, relationships, relationships. That was the message I was given as a first-year principal over 20 years ago by my line manager, former Area Supervisor, Damien Barker. In the last 20 years there has been a greater emphasis on compliance and accountability. This has often created great tensions for school leaders and teachers as they try to balance building positive relationships with the many protocols, practices, procedures, processes and policies. Even the Australian government acknowledges that there is too much red tape for teachers and school leaders to manage. They commissioned a review to identify ways to increase the practices to enhance teaching and learning and minimise the burden of compliance and administration (AITSL 2020). Whether any of the recommendations will make a difference in the lives of teachers and school leaders is too early to evaluate at the time of printing.

Strong leaders need to do what is right. It takes a strong leader to identify an injustice within protocols or accepted practices and challenge them. Without such leadership many injustices would still exist. Strong leaders need the practices, procedures, protocols, processes and policies within which to build positive, harmonious relationships. Balance is necessary.

BIBLIOGRAPHY

Age Discrimination Act 2004.

American Federation of Teachers (2007) *Building Parent-Teacher Relationships*, American Federation of Teachers, Washington, DC.

Andrikidis P (director) (2016) *Alex and Eve* [motion picture], Magicbox Entertainment, Australia.

Australian Council for Educational Research (ACER) (2012) *National School Improvement Tool*, Australian Council for Educational Research, Australia.

Australian Council for Educational Research (ACER) (2012) *School & System Improvement*, accessed 12 April 2022. https://www.acer.org/au/school-improvement/improvement-tools/national-school-improvement-tool

Australian Council for Educational Research (ACER) (2022) *Assessment*, accessed 12 April 2022. https://www.acer.org/au/assessment

Australian Curriculum, Assessment and Reporting Authority (ACARA) (2020) *Australian Curriculum*, accessed 12 April 2022. https://www.acara.edu.au/

Australian Curriculum, Assessment and Reporting Authority (ACARA) (2021) *National Assessment Program – Literacy and Numeracy,* accessed 12 April 2022. https://www.nap.edu.au/

Australian Education Act 2013.

Australian Human Rights Commission (2014) *A Quick Guide to Australian Discrimination Laws*, accessed 12 April 2022. https://humanrights.gov.au/our-work/employers/quick-guide-australian-discrimination-laws

Australian Institute for Teaching and School Leadership (AITSL) (2020) *Shifting the Balance: Increasing the Focus on Teaching and Learning by Reducing the Burden of Compliance and Administration – Review to Reduce Tape for Teachers and School Leaders*, accessed 12 April 2022. https://pages.aitsl.edu.au/red-tape/review-to-reduce-red-tape-for-teachers-and-school-leaders

Barker G (director) (2020) *Sergio* [motion picture], Black Rabbit Media, Anima Pictures, Itapoan, United States.

Brown B (2020) *A Courageous Approach to Feedback*, accessed 12 April 2022. https://brenebrown.com/collections/a-courageous-approach-to-feedback/

Chbosky S (director) (2017) *Wonder* [motion picture], Lionsgate, Mandeville Films, Participant Media, Walden Media, TIK Films, United States.

Covey S (2020) *7 Habits of Highly Effective People*, Simon & Schuster, Australia.

Crews B (2021) *Twelve Rules for Living a Better Life,* Harper Collins Publishers, Australia.

Disability Discrimination Act 1992.

Disability Standards of Education 2005.

Dweck C (2014) *Developing a Growth Mindset with Carol Dweck* [video], accessed 12 April 2022. https://www.youtube.com/watch?v=hiiEeMN7vbQ

Education Council (2019) *Alice Springs (Mparntwe) Education Declaration*, accessed 12 April 2022. https://www.dese.gov.au/alice-springs-mparntwe-education-declaration/resources/alice-springs-mparntwe-education-declaration

Epstein D (2019) *Range*, Pan Macmillan, Australia.

Farrelly P (director) (2018) *Green Book* [motion picture], Participant Media, DreamWorks Pictures, Reliance Entertainment, Innisfree Pictures, Cinetic Media, Alibaba Pictures, Unites States.

Gladwell M (2008) *Outliers*, Penguin Books UK, Great Britain.

Grentell M (director) (2018) *The Merger* [motion picture], Anne Robinson, Mark Grentell, Damian Callinan, Australia.

Grinder M (2011) *A Healthy Classroom*, Hawker Brownlow Education, Australia.

Hancock JL (director) (2009) *The Blind Side* [motion picture], Alcon Entertainment, United States.

Hargreaves A and O'Connor MT (2018) *Leading Collaborative Professionalism*, Centre for Strategic Education, Seminar Series paper 274, Melbourne, Australia.

Harris M (2022) *Our High-Impact Strategies that Lead Student Learning*, School News Issue 23, Term 1. Multimedia, Noosaville, Australia.

Hattie J (2008) *Visible Learning*, Taylor & Francis Ltd, Great Britain.

Herek S (director) (1995) *Mr Holland's Opus* [motion picture], Hollywood Pictures, Interscope Communications, PolyGram Filmed Entertainment, United States.

House of Representatives Standing Committee on Education and Training (2002) *Boys: Getting it Right – Report on the Inquiry into the Education of Boys*, Chapter 5, accessed 12 April 2022. www.aphref.aph.gov.au_house_committee_edt_eofb_report_chapter5.pdf

Jordan M (n.d.) "Michael Jordan Quotes", *Goodreads*, accessed 12 April 2022. https://www.goodreads.com/author/quotes/16823.Michael_Jordan

Komasa J (director) (2020) *The Hater* [motion picture], Naima Film, dFlights, TVN, Canal+, Coloroffon, Poland.

Lang K (2021) "State Government accuses of gender pay equality fail over Katarina Carroll wage" *Courier Mail*, accessed 12 April 2022. https://www.couriermail.com.au/news/queensland/state-government-accuses-of-gender-pay-equality-fail-over-katarina-carroll-wage/news-story/6a41939ec1d9adcf48aedbecf5578898?amp

Leder M (director) (2018) *On the Basis of Sex* [motion picture], Focus Features, Participant Media, Robert Cort Productions, Alibaba Pictures, United States.

Lotzof M (2017) *Legal but Harmful: Insights to Trump, Tribalism and Change – Beyond Good and Evil*, Strategic Change and E-Tram Pty Ltd Imprint.

Luhrmann, B (director) (2008) *Australia* [motion picture], Bazmark Films Australia; Ingenious Media; ScreenWest, Australia

McCormack G (2020) LinkedIn post.

Melfi T (director) (2016) *Hidden Figures* [motion picture], Fox 2000 Pictures, Chernin Entertainment, Levantine Films, United States.

Morrison S (2021) Press conference transcript, 8 January, Parliament House, accessed 12 April 2022. https://www.pm.gov.au/media/press-conference-australian-parliament-house-14

Narragunnawali: Reconciliation in Education (n.d.) *Terminology Guide*, accessed 12 April 2022. https://www.narragunnawali.org.au/about/terminology-guide

Oberthur A (2021) *Are You Ready for School?*, Amba Press, Melbourne, Australia.

Parker D (2021) LinkedIn post.

Parker A (2019) *The Negotiator's Toolkit*, 5th edition, Peak Performance Development, Australia.

Pierson R (2013) *Every Kid Needs a Champion* [video], accessed 12 April 2022. https://www.ted.com/talks/rita_pierson_every_kid_needs_a_champion?language=en

Privacy Act 1988

Queensland Curriculum and Assessment Authority (2021) https://www.qcaa.qld.edu.au/

Racial Discrimination Act 1975.

Sex Discrimination Act 1984.

Sharratt L and Fullan M (2012) *Putting Faces on the Data: What Great Leaders Do!,* Corwin, Australia.

Shetty J (2020) *Think Like a Monk,* Harper Thorsons, London.

Sinek S (n.d.) Instagram post.

Sorkin A (director) (1992) *A Few Good Men* [motion picture], Castle Rock Entertainment, United States.

Sweatman J and Oberthur A (2020) *Survivor Guide to Homeschooling,* LinkedIn post.

University of Texas (n.d.) *How Much of Communication Is Nonverbal?,* accessed 12 April 2022. https://online.utpb.edu/about-us/articles/communication/how-much-of-communication-is-nonverbal/

Voight A (2021) *Canaries in the Classroom,* accessed 12 April 2022. https://www.linkedin.com/pulse/canaries-classroom-adam-voigt/?trackingId=fBexbLS8Lg%2BokDsnvetGyQ%3D%3D

Weir P (director) (1989) *Dead Poets Society* [motion picture], Touchstone Pictures, United States.

APPENDIX A:

Conditions for Learning Diagram

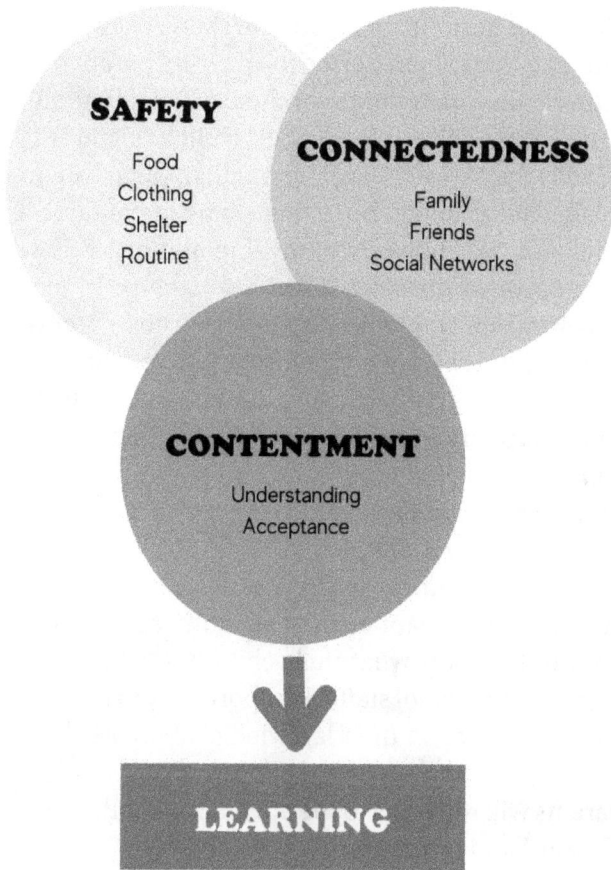

SAFETY

Food
Clothing
Shelter
Routine

CONNECTEDNESS

Family
Friends
Social Networks

CONTENTMENT

Understanding
Acceptance

LEARNING

APPENDIX B:

Formula for Trust and Collaboration

3 + 3 + 3 + 5 + 2

When a child comes home from school and shares their recollection about something that has happened during the day, the parent has the choice of *three* responses from which they may choose in dealing with their child's concern. If the parent believes what their child has said is 100% accurate and factual, AND they are not happy about that, then the parent has some options. The *first option* might be to ring, email or contact the school staff and "explode". Not preferable but not uncommon. This will not build a relationship between the school and the parents. In fact it will break down the relationship. The *second option* is for the parents to say to the child "Thanks very much I believe your story but toughen up, grow up and be more resilient". This in effect is brushing the child aside. They're not giving them the support and empowerment that they need and deserve. The *third option* is for the parents to listen to the child cautiously and then choose one of three responses, and then one of three questions which they should ask the school staff.

The *first question* is simply to say to the school staff when they have the opportunity – "What happened at school?" regarding this particular matter. They would report what their child has said about the incident and they then give the school staff the opportunity to respond. This simply allows the staff to reflect on their knowledge of the issue without getting defensive. They are simply sharing information with the parents. At that point the parents will reflect as to the accuracy of both stories so that they can move forward and in supporting their child.

The *second question* the parents may choose to use is – "What is the schools policy or protocols or procedures regarding (whatever)?". For example if a child comes home with an injury and the parents were not notified before the child got home and that caused distress for the parents, they may simply contact the school and ask very politely and calmly what is the schools policy and protocols and procedures for notifying parents regarding injuries? With that information they are in a position to judge whether or not the school followed the process and protocols or whether or not the school has let them down.

The *third question* at the parents may choose to use is "What can we as parents and teachers do in working together for my child's education?". This highlights the need for collaboration. It highlights the importance of the parents and teachers working together and providing a common vision of education for the children.

When a parent comes and expresses some concerns to a teacher, the teacher can easily get defensive. If we are in a position to build a culture of trust and collaboration between parents and teachers, then I believe there are only three questions that teachers need to ask parents in response to any of the concerns.

The *first question* is simply "What do you need?". This means that the parents need to reflect upon the purpose as to why they are coming and having a conversation with the teacher and what they hope to achieve by having a conversation. So by the teacher asking the question: what do you need? the parents sits back and reflects and thinks "Am I here to share information?" Or am I here because I want a resolution to a problem? Or am I here because I want some advice and I hope the teacher can give me some advice about a particular issue. Or am I here simply to gather information and a better understanding about what's happening in the school. As soon as the teacher asks the question "What do you need?" they are in fact responding to the importance of the parents' query. This adds value to the parents question and hence the parent feels that they are important and that you are validating their query and it and will be addressed.

The *second question* that teachers could ask parents when they come for an interview or meeting is "What do you imagine that would look like in our classroom or in our school?" So when a parent comes and asks for a request for something to be achieved or something to be done, when the teacher asks the parent "What you think that would look like?", it puts the emphasis back on the parent to try articulate the practical application for their query to be implemented in the classroom or school setting. When the question is asked, parents are often able to sit back and think what they're asking may not be practical, it may not be sustainable, it may not be possible to impose something on the teachers. A lightbulb moment may occur and the parents may then reframe their query or question to be more practical and realistic.

The *third question* that teachers can ask parents is "Is there anything else you'd like to ask or say or tell me before we close the meeting?" This simply gives the parents the chance to reflect and to ensure that their needs have been met and both parties can walk away content that they have been heard. So it's a simple technique which allows teachers to close off the conversation. It also allows the parents some closure. They have had the opportunity to express their concerns, and had the opportunity to be heard. There may be a resolution which meets their needs and if there's not, then parents may choose to take their concerns further, to a member of the school's leadership team. Hopefully the same pattern of questioning can be employed.

Parents now have these questions, so when you visit a school to make an enquiry, you can reframe your questions around this model even if the teachers don't use the questions to direct your conversation.

When a parent goes to their child's school they usually approach the teachers or the principal for one of *five* reasons. Once they are asked "What do you need?" it helps them reflect on why they have gone to the school.

The *first reason* why parents go to school is to simply share information, good or bad. It might be to give information, to give praise or simply to get something off their chest, to express their opinion and once they have expressed their concerns about whatever, they're happy. This the first reason for engaging with schools.

The *second reason* parents may come to a school is to seek information, context or history. They just want to understand the history so that they get a better grasp of why the system exists and how long the system has existed. They are just seeking information, context or history.

The *third reason* parents may go to school to talk to the principal or a teacher may be to offer a solution. Parents may have expertise in a field that may add value to the school. The principal often calls upon parent expertise in an advisory capacity. This model is relevant when parents have a particular skills set that can benefit the school community. It is also a reason why parents may be invited to join school boards, as they bring expertise to the table.

The *fourth reason* may be that the parents are asking the school for a resolution or a solution to the particular issue. If the processes are reviewed and can be improved then a solution may be possible. Solutions are not always possible or resolutions may not always give the parents their desired outcome. It is important to remember that principals and school leaders make decisions in the best interests of all (or the majority) of families and students. The principal also has the "big picture" in mind, whereas the parents only have to worry about their children. This is seeking a resolution or a solution to their particular problem.

Similar to the fourth reason is the *final reason* parents may engage with schools – and that is to seek advice from staff. This model requires the parents to own the implementation of the advice. This highlights collaboration as the parents request advice from the staff, and then the parents have to act on it.

I would encourage teachers and principals to simply ask the question what does the parent need when they come in to have a conversation with a member of staff. Once the parent can articulate what they need then the teacher or the principal is in the position to understand the rationale for visiting and hence can tailor their response to meet the parents' needs understand the context as to why they're there. It's not easy but it's worth the journey. Good luck!

When teachers respond to any parent request the teacher should filter their response with these *two criteria*: is the response **SUSTAINABLE** and **REALISTIC**. If the teacher's response meets these criteria then it may be a viable option. If the response desired by the parents from the teacher does not meet these criteria then it would be advisable to rethink the options. It may be necessary to revisit the first question from teacher to parents – what do you need? This may prompt the parents to rethink their desired outcomes.

The formula for building a culture of trust and collaboration is $3 + 3 + 3 + 5 + 2$.

APPENDIX C:

Formula for Trust Diagram

3 Responses
Believe
Dismiss
Listen

2 Criteria
For Teacher
Commitment

5 Reasons
Parents
Engage With
School Staff

Child

3 Questions
Teachers Ask
Parents

3 Questions
Parents Ask
Teachers

APPENDIX D:

Examples of School Issues

Summary of a sample of school issues that could be managed under each criteria.

Improving learning and well-being of students, staff and families	• Teaching cycle – planning, teaching, assessing, reporting • School reviews, using the National School Improvement Tool
Safety	• Excursions • Electrical testing and tagging • Risk assessments for events • Dress code for staff (suitable for role)
Transparency	• Staffing appointments to school • Assigning staff to roles within a school • Following up incidents with parents
Interests of the Majority	• Playground duty roster • Specialist timetables • Carnivals
Fairness	• Responding to staff, student and family needs • Differentiation, individual needs
Realistic and Sustainable	• Responding to staff, student and family wants
Cost Benefits	• Building programs • Staffing levels
Legal Requirements	• Communication within school community • High-quality education for all students

APPENDIX D:

Examples of School Issues

Summary of a sample of school issues that could be managed under each criteria.

Improving learning and well-being of students, staff and families.	• Teaching – lesson planning • Teaching – assessing, reporting • School reviews using the National School Improvement Tool
Safety.	• Behaviour • Bullying, teasing and tagging • Risk assessment, for events • Dress code for staff (suitability)
Transparency	• Staffing appointments to school • Assigning staff to roles within a school • Following up incidents with parents
Interests of the Majority	• Playground duty rosters • Sport at lunchtimes • Carnivals
Fairness	• Responding to staff, student and family needs • Differentiation, individual needs
Realistic and Sustainable	• Responding to staff, student and family wants
Cost Benefits	• Building program • Staffing levels
Legal Requirements	• Compliance with school policy • High quality education for all students